ASSESSING STUDENT PORTFOLIOS FOR COLLEGE CREDIT

Chari A. Leader Kelley, PhD

The Council for Adult and Experiential Learning
Chicago

For Shawn, Carissa, and Kevin who inspire me every day.

The Council for Adult & Experiential Learning
55 East Monroe Street, Suite 2710
Chicago, Illinois 60603
www.cael.org

© 2017 The Council for Adult and Experiential Learning (CAEL)

ISBN 978-1-5249-1343-4

Manufactured in the United States of America
10 9 8 7 6 5 4 3 2

Assessing
Student Portfolios
for College Credit:

*Everything you need to know
to ensure academic integrity
in portfolio assessment*

Chari A. Leader Kelley, PhD

CONTENTS

ACKNOWLEDGEMENTS

The author wishes to acknowledge the many contributions made by the expert professionals at CAEL, including Kristen Himmerick, Scott Campbell, Donna Younger, and Becky Klein-Collins. Special thanks to Larry Kelley for his ongoing support and encouragement.

FOREWORD

Much has changed since the Council for Adult and Experiential Learning (CAEL) published *Prior Learning Portfolios: A Representative Collection* in 2008. Prior learning assessment (PLA) is now considered to be a mainstream method for assessing prior learning. As the sources of college-level learning have become more diverse and accessible, the centrality of assessing that learning has also grown. This explosion in the sources of knowledge, ranging from industry-recognized credentials to MOOCs and other online courses, is challenging leaders within higher education to recognize the learning in new ways. Furthermore, the use of portfolio assessment has been elevated from a tool used by an isolated department on the edge of campus to an important strategy that supports retention, persistence, and adult student success. State systems and workforce development entities are also utilizing prior learning assessment strategies to help jumpstart their economic competitiveness initiatives, targeting those individuals with some college and no degree.

Chari Leader Kelley is the perfect choice to author this publication. As a nationally recognized practitioner of and thought-leader on PLA, Leader Kelley brings creativity and wisdom to the process. As one of the first Vice Presidents of LearningCounts, CAEL's online portfolio assessment service, she has honed her perspectives through context-specific PLA experiences in hundreds of colleges, universities, and state systems of higher education.

Translating, deciphering, bridging, and/or equating what a learner knows and can do in order to receive college credit can be tricky, daunting, and even overwhelming. Without integrity, the process can undermine the value of the credentials it seeks to make accessible. At its best, the process can provide an academically responsible, motivating, and meaningful bridge to postsecondary education. If taken to scale, this process can unleash unrealized talent and light a pathway toward more meaningful personal and professional lives for millions of individuals, especially adults with some college and no degree.

Unlike many books on higher education that are written with an emphasis on theoretical constructs without concrete examples, Leader Kelly includes actual student portfolios and discusses how to effectively assess students' portfolios. She also addresses the myths that have grown up around prior learning assessment, allaying the fears of faculty and administrators through concrete evidence of the value of using portfolio assessments to help adult students succeed. Building upon the foundation offered in *Prior Learning Portfolios: A Representative Collection*, Leader Kelley has focused the new edition on dual perspectives, that of the student and of the assessor. Her expertise in transfer and articulation policies, focused on college credit for adult students, is apparent.

This book provides a valuable resource for a wide range of individuals. Administrators and practitioners will benefit from the pragmatic and accessible information embedded in the multiple portfolio examples. Faculty members can view examples of portfolios that mirror their own syllabi, providing evidence of learning through a written narrative and supportive documentation. The portfolio examples demonstrate how students meet and exceed the learning outcomes for real college courses.

As a former college dean whose responsibilities included PLA, I recognize that building a culture of evidence requires perseverance and vision on the part of all members of the institutional team. *Assessing Student Portfolios for College Credit: Everything You Need to Know to Ensure Academic Integrity in Portfolio Assessment* offers the foundational theories as well as clear, well-defined steps for the creation and implementation of portfolio assessment as an integral offering in prior learning assessment. The tools outlined in this book set the stage for adult students to succeed in college, the workplace, and in life.

This updated edition of *Assessing Student Portfolios for College Credit* signals CAEL's continued leadership as the standard bearer for quality and excellence in assessing learning and recognizing what adult students know and can do.

Scott A. Campbell, PhD
Vice President for Higher Education
CAEL

INTRODUCTION

Prior learning assessment (PLA) is opportunity. It's an opportunity first posited as a social justice strategy in the 1960s, leveling the field for those coming to higher education later than those with more privileged backgrounds. **It's about access**—to a college degree, to the middle class, to career success, and to the American Dream. It has long fought to become part of mainstream higher education, but mainstream higher education has had no interest in engaging in a conversation about PLA, until now.

Prior learning assessment helps students earn college credit for college-level learning and skills acquired outside of the traditional college classroom. Portfolio assessment is the most misunderstood PLA method. The purpose of this book is to demystify portfolio assessment while providing everything you need to know about portfolio assessment to ensure academic integrity in your portfolio program.

Portfolio Assessment's New-Found Popularity. Over 40 years since its first application, portfolio assessment has emerged as an important strategy for better serving adult learners There are a number of reasons for this (see Figure 1):

- **Changing student demographics.** *"The 'traditional' college student—young, white, male, wealthy—is a thing of the past"* (Williams 2014). In fact, many of the "traditional" descriptors of college students have changed. Today's college student is more likely to be working; not living in a dorm. She may also be the first in her family to go to college. She has adult responsibilities including possibly having dependents, bills to pay, and a job. These life circumstances make her commitment to college subject to more stressors than college students of previous generations.

Many students today are students who have stopped or dropped out of college previously and now have years of work experience and real world skills. Moreover, today's students are more likely to need financial aid. Students who earn credit via portfolio assessment are able to reduce the time it takes to complete their degrees, save tuition dollars, thus reducing their student debt loads. According to the National Center for Education Statistics (NCES), demographic changes projected as far into the future as 2023 show even more growth in the prevalence of older students:

> *In recent years, the percentage increase in the number of students age 25 and over who enrolled in degree-granting institutions has been similar to the*

PLA Methods

- National for-credit exams, such as CLEP (College-Level Examination Program from the College Board), DSSTs (DANTES Subject Standardized Tests), AP (The College Board's Advanced Placement Exams), and UExcel Exams (national standardized examinations from Excelsior College)

- American Council on Education (ACE)–evaluated military education and training programs

- ACE-evaluated corporate and employer training and education programs

- National College Credit Recommendation Service (NCCRS)-evaluated training and education programs

- Faculty-developed challenge exams

- Portfolio assessment (individualized assessment)

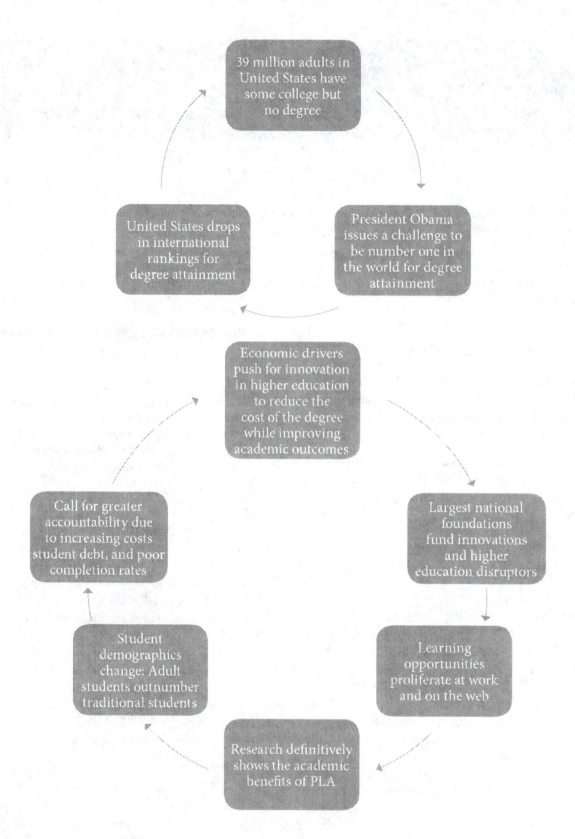

FIGURE 1. *The Dynamics of Portfolio Assessment Usage. This figure illustrates the factors leading to the greater use of portfolio assessment.*

*percentage increase in the number of younger students, but the rate of increase is expected to be higher for students age 25 and over than for younger students in the coming years. Between 2000 and 2012, the enrollment of students under age 25 and the enrollment of those age 25 and over both increased by 35 percent. **From 2012 to 2023, however, NCES projects the rate of increase for students under age 25 to be 12 percent, compared with 20 percent for students age 25 and over [emphasis added].** (Snyder and Dillow 2015)*

- **Call for greater accountability.** Policy makers from the White House to state houses throughout the United States have been critical of higher education, as costs have risen faster than inflation over the past 20 years. Rhetoric tends to point to a need for greater transparency, for developing new approaches for 21st-century students, and for putting more focus on student outcomes (particularly graduation rates). PLA can be an important tool in helping students make faster progress toward attaining their educational goals.

  Portfolio assessment helps students leverage their prior learning toward degree requirements so that they do not need to take courses in subjects where they are already competent. Higher education critics have long questioned higher education policies that limit recognition of prior learning, most notably in credit transfer and articulation.

  A case in point is the Tennessee Higher Education Commission (THEC) Outcomes-Based Funding Formula. The outcomes-based funding formula rewards "…institutions for the production of outcomes that further the educational attainment and productivity goals of the state Master Plan" (Tennessee Higher Education Commission 2015). As a result, institutions are incentivized to enroll, retain, and graduate more students, particularly adults. Incentives are awarded to students progressing past certain credit hour attainment benchmarks. Therefore, students who earn PLA credit are able to meet the benchmarks sooner, triggering increased funding.

- **Research on the benefits of PLA.** CAEL's 2010 landmark longitudinal research study *Fueling the Race to Postsecondary Success* (Klein-Collins 2010) moved PLA front and center in discussions on improving degree completion and ways to better serve adult and other nontraditional students. The major study tracked 64,750 students (age 25 or older) from 48 different colleges and universities to determine the differences in academic outcomes for students with PLA credits and those without PLA credits on their transcripts.

  The students in the study with any form of PLA credits on their transcripts were more likely to have completed their degrees during the seven-year period than students without PLA credits. Further, PLA students who did not complete degrees during that period were more likely to be still enrolled and to have taken more courses than their non-PLA counterparts.

- **Importance of postsecondary education and training for adults to keep the economy moving.** In 1990, the United States ranked number one in the world for four-year degree attainment among 25 to 34 year olds, while today the United States does not even make it into the top 10 list of O.E.C.D. countries' higher education attainment statistics, now ranking 19th in the world.[1] In 2009, President Obama issued a national challenge to move the United States back to number one by 2020 in order to assure US global competitiveness and a more inclusive academy.[2]

  This challenge, now at the heart of Lumina Foundation's funding for postsecondary education, has led to the adoption of new strategies to improve postsecondary attainment. Some

---

[1] Retrieved from www.oecd.org/edu/EAG-Interim-report.pdf on November 23, 2015.
[2] Retrieved from https://www.whitehouse.gov/issues/education/higher-education on September 5, 2015.

of these strategies include outreach to adults with some college and no degrees to re-engage in higher education; investing resources to place greater emphasis on PLA and portfolio assessment (with its funding of *LearningCounts.org*, CAEL's online portfolio assessment service); and funding innovations, such as competency-based education, among many other projects.

- **Technology developments.** Improvements in technology have greatly enhanced portfolio assessment. With digital portfolios, newly completed portfolios can be routed to faculty by e-mail and assessed online. It is now easier than ever before to track portfolios, assessor results, and archive successful portfolios, should questions regarding the credit awards occur later. Technology is also making it easier to track student academic outcomes for PLA generally, and its methods more specifically.

- **New sources of postsecondary learning.** The Internet has hundreds of thousands of opportunities to learn, but not necessarily to earn college credits. When students participate in MOOCs (massive online open courses) offered by the most prestigious colleges and universities in the country, they do not earn credit. Others are earning digital badges for knowledge gained through self-directed learning, training, and volunteer efforts. Still more are engaging in professional development and other educational pursuits, such as open educational resources like Khan Academy. All of this learning might be eligible for college credit, if the learning aligns with credit offerings in a student's academic program of study. Portfolio assessment offers the most flexibility in certifying these new sources of learning.

Today, thousands of students challenge themselves and the higher education system by developing portfolios and submitting them for assessments. Credit awards can range from credit for 1 course (3 credits) to credit for 10 courses (30 credits). When done correctly, all of these credits will count toward the students' degree requirements. Imagine how much time could be saved if the student is attending part-time in the evenings and earns six credit hours with portfolio assessment. That student, who may typically take one course per semester, has just shaved two semesters off her/his timeline to completion and saved six credit hours of tuition.

Perhaps the most exciting aspect of portfolio assessment is the *sheer joy students feel* when they are successful in earning credit for what they know. The reinforcement that their knowledge (gained outside of academia) is worthy of college credit and is now applicable to their degrees, inspires a motivation that cannot be quantified – the motivation to complete the degree and attain an important life goal.

Using This Book

This book is organized in a way that lets you examine real student portfolios from different perspectives. In chapter one, after reading about the history of portfolio assessment and the mythology surrounding it, you will be able to view pieces of the portfolio with Kolb's Learning Theory in mind. In chapter two, you will learn about all of the elements of a portfolio with student examples. Chapter three dives into the importance of clear learning outcomes as well as how to recognize the components of an excellent portfolio. Chapter four provides a practitioner's perspective, while chapter five focuses on assuring quality in a portfolio assessment program as well as assessment rubrics. Chapter six gives you an opportunity to practice assessing a student portfolio. Frequently asked questions are addressed in Chapter seven. The book wraps up with a chapter discussing the future of portfolio assessment, particularly as it relates to the bigger picture of competency-based education and emerging frameworks.

The book includes actual student portfolios seeking credit for the following courses:

- BA-390 Purchasing Management
- BBM-320 Business Communications
- PARA-2010 Introduction to Paralegal Studies
- LEAD-310 Leadership Theory and Practice II
- PAD-332 Municipal Government Operations
- MGMT-3143 Human Resource Management
- CIS-175 Introduction to Networking

Assessing Student Portfolios for College Credit covers everything you need to know to ensure academic integrity in portfolio assessment.

A Student's Point of View

Portfolio assessment was the bridge I needed to earn my baccalaureate degree. With many years of experience in advertising, marketing, sales, public relations, and management, I thought it would be easy to earn credits for my experiential learning. But I was wrong about the "easy" part. It was actually a very arduous, time-consuming, and often tedious project that taxed my organizational skills and filled all available surfaces of my home with piles of papers, notes, and textbooks. Was it easy? No. Was it worthwhile? Absolutely!

Here's what I learned from going through the process of developing a portfolio:

1. There was much more to me, and my knowledge base, than I could have ever known without this experience. Organizing my experiential learning, skills, and knowledge against courses ranging from Introduction to Public Relations to Principles of Management helped me to reflect upon my experiences from a totally new vantage point. Reflection was something I never had time for until I started my portfolio.

2. Reviewing the various textbooks associated with my targeted courses for the portfolio was very interesting. I read about things I already knew but didn't know there was a name for what I had been doing! Linking the experience with the applicable theories elevated my learning to a whole new level that was really exciting for me. It motivated me to keep going forward. Building the portfolio (for 33 credits) took me about six months to complete. My learning was refreshed and I felt empowered.

3. Collecting the artifacts, letters of verification, and other documentation was the tedious part. Finding old supervisors and asking them to write the letters took time. Digging up old documents was like excavating many years of past hard work.

4. Writing the learning narratives while ensuring I touched on all of the topics of the courses and learning objectives or outcomes took many weeks. I was working full-time, attending classes at night, and working on my portfolios. All of this was happening against the backdrop of three children who needed my attention.

I remember when it was finally completed, and I handed the portfolio (all in paper form at that time) over to the office of the Vice President for Academic Affairs. I was so incredibly nervous as to how the portfolio would be "judged" and if, in fact, I could earn enough credits to reduce my time to degree by years!

After what seemed like forever, I received my portfolio back, and I was delighted to have earned 30 credit hours. It was like winning the lottery. I was college material! I could earn a degree! And, so I did—as a first generation college student. I graduated and went on to earn a master's and my doctorate. If I hadn't done the portfolio, I likely would have ended up as another adult learner who had life circumstances get in the way of completing the degree. I was lucky my college had a strong portfolio assessment program.

Chari Leader Kelley

CHAPTER 1

TRIALS AND TRIBULATIONS

A Brief History

Portfolio assessment started as a three-year research project of the Educational Testing Service (ETS) along with 10 colleges and universities in 1974. The experiment, funded by a grant from the Carnegie Foundation, was the result of a series of recommendations made by the Commission on Non-Traditional Study (sponsored by ETS and the College Board) in 1971. ETS was interested in determining if a person's learning from outside of the college setting could be evaluated for college credit with rigor strong enough to be reliable and valid. The CAEL Project—CAEL originally stood for the Cooperative Assessment of Experiential Learning—conducted research in testing portfolio implementation models at 10 institutions (Hart and Hickerson 2009).

The Project produced 27 publications and over 50 reports. National conferences were held to disseminate the research findings, building awareness and adoption for portfolio assessment. By 1977, 270 colleges and universities were part of the CAEL Project (Hart and Hickerson 2009). The outcome of the research was the determination that experiential learning, or nontraditional learning, could be assessed with academic rigor for college credit. The Project became CAEL—with CAEL now standing for the Council for the Advancement of Experiential Learning—organized to assure quality assessment of learning outcomes, including those from work experience, and portfolio assessment specifically. See Appendix A for a PLA timeline.

1974 CAEL Project Institutions

- Antioch College (now Antioch University)
- Community College of Vermont
- El Paso Community College
- Empire State College
- Florida International University
- Framingham State College
- Minnesota Metropolitan State College (now Metropolitan State University)
- New College, University of Alabama
- San Francisco State College (now San Francisco State University)
- Thomas A. Edison State College (now Thomas Edison State University)

Today CAEL, The Council for Adult and Experiential Learning, is a well-respected national organization headquartered in Chicago. CAEL's membership includes 310 institutional members, 13 organizational members, 22 international members, 30 system members, and 205 individual members devoted to improving recognition of adult learning. Over the past 40 years, PLA usage at American colleges and universities has blossomed, particularly for two methods: testing for credit and recognizing ACE-evaluated military training and education programs. Portfolio assessment, on the other hand, has been slower to take hold. The reasons for its slow uptake were primarily rooted in faculty concerns about its validity, misunderstandings regarding credit awards, and the overall cost to administer portfolio assessment programs. This chapter will explore the mythology around portfolio assessment as well as the stimulators to growth in portfolio assessment during the past decade.

Portfolio Assessment Overview

Portfolio assessment is an academic service through which any student can align experiential learning with college curricula by allowing faculty subject matter experts to determine if the student's learning is comparable and equivalent to college-level learning. This process results in an assessment that yields a "credit or no credit decision." Successful portfolio assessment students earn credits for their portfolios. Table 1 describes the necessary elements of a portfolio.

TABLE 1. *COMPONENTS OF A LEARNING PORTFOLIO*

Portfolio Components	What They Look Like	What They Mean
Course Match or Aligning Learning with Institutionally Defined Competencies	The student selects a course that aligns with her/his learning. The student may even select a series of courses within a discipline or from various disciplines for which to prepare portfolios. Portfolios are usually organized by discipline or by a single course per portfolio. Institutionally defined competencies may be organized by courses or standalone. Students can demonstrate equivalent competencies to earn credit.	The course descriptions start the student on a path to articulating her/his learning according to the course description. Course descriptions will either rule a course in as a possible credit opportunity or rule it out.
Course Syllabus	Once a student picks the course, best practice indicates the student should find the most recent syllabus for the course at her/his institution.	The syllabus is literally the road map or "course outline" for the student in preparing and documenting learning. If the syllabus is organized by outcomes, objectives, competencies, or topics, the student will articulate her/his learning accordingly; aligning experiences and extracting the learning outcomes.
Introduction or Overview	The student provides an overview/introduction to the assessor/reader. This section is generally two to three paragraphs that sets the context for the assessment.	The student essentially introduces her/himself, describing how the student came to know the information and some personal information that helps the assessor understand who the student is and why they chose to write a portfolio.
Learning Narrative and/or Learning Demonstration	The student must write about her/his learning as it aligns with the learning outcomes, objectives, competencies, or topics of the course. The student must write at the college level (APA style or whatever academic style the institution prefers), explain how the information was learned, how the learning relates to new situations or in different contexts, and how the learning might be used in the future. Learning narratives tend to be similar to a term paper, generally 10-15 pages long.	The heart of the portfolio, the learning narrative must align with the course syllabus. If a demonstration makes more sense, such as for a skill from advanced manufacturing, then the student can either make an appointment for an assessor to view the student performing the skill or submit a video or other form of demonstration. Assessors will carefully examine how the learning aligns, if it is college level, as well as how well the student is able to discuss any underlying theoretical constructs.

(Continued)

Portfolio Components	What They Look Like	What They Mean
Structured Interview	Relatively new to portfolio assessment, some institutions are experimenting with a structured interview. The interview, conducted by the assessor or assessors, is constructed in a way that enables the student to discuss her/his learning in response to structured questions and prompts.	The structured interview relieves the student of the burden of writing an extensive learning narrative. Like a demonstration, the assessors are able to determine the breadth and depth of learning based upon the interview in a way similar to defending a dissertation.
Documentation or Artifacts	Documentation might include videos, work products, published work, certificates, CEU awards, and letters of verification from employers or experts attesting to the learning.	The student must prove that what he or she is saying is true by including documentation. Proving the case is essential to the credit award. Authentic documentation supporting the student's learning statements is required.
Rubric	The rubric allows the student to know how the portfolio will be assessed. Knowing in advance what the criteria are for the assessment is important for student success.	The rubric ensures a fair, transparent, and well-documented assessment. Use of the rubric helps to ensure inter-rater reliability and validity in the assessment.
Assessor Feedback	Assessors should provide both positive and constructive feedback, whether the portfolio ultimately is credit worthy or not.	Assessor feedback ensures learning continues from portfolio development through credit determination. Assessment is integral to learning.

Dispelling the Myths

The myths surrounding portfolio assessment have been detrimental to faculty adoption of the academic process. Many of these myths started with just one faculty member at an institution who didn't understand portfolio assessment or maybe saw it done incorrectly. Over the years, the voice of that one faculty member may be magnified exponentially, preventing new faculty members from having the opportunity to understand and embrace portfolio assessment as an important assessment tool.

MYTH: Portfolio assessment lures students with the promise of easy credits.

REALITY: Some institutions use the availability of portfolio assessment as a recruiting tool, particularly for adults. When done correctly, credits are never promised or assured in advance of the student actually completing a portfolio. In fact, academic advising is critical so students do not seek credit that may be duplicative or may not actually meet a degree requirement. In the past, some proprietary schools over emphasized portfolio assessment—often referred to as "credit for life experience"—in national advertising. This practice has caused faculty to question the legitimacy of the process. However, when done correctly, portfolio assessment is not only rigorous but also aligns the student's actual learning with the course syllabus for outcome-to-outcome assessment. Credit can only be awarded when the student demonstrates the same learning outcomes in the portfolio as a student who has passed the course with a "C" grade or better.

MYTH: Portfolio assessment cannot have the same rigor as student experience in a course.

REALITY: There are always assertions, such as "Students doing portfolios cannot benefit from the robust discussions in my classroom; therefore, they won't understand the nuances of the subject matter." The fact is that while portfolio students miss classroom discussions, they do need to attain the same learning outcomes or competencies as the students who participate in classroom discussions. If a course outcome is that students can discuss the nuances of the subject matter, then the portfolio student must articulate these nuances in the portfolio. The rigor of a portfolio might even be tougher, given students must address all learning outcomes at a "C" grade or better. On the other hand, classroom students may be able to address *certain outcomes* in exams and not address others while still earning a "C" or better for the course.

MYTH: Portfolio assessment is subjective and inconsistent.

REALITY: Of all of the misconceptions of portfolio assessment, this is the most damaging assumption. When done properly, portfolio assessment is as rigorous as the articulated outcomes for the course to which learning is being aligned. In other words, if the course syllabus clearly states what is expected of students—whether in terms of learning outcomes, objectives, topics, or competencies—then portfolio students must align their learning accordingly. Portfolio students must demonstrate the same learning outcomes, at a "C" grade or better, as students who pass the course in a traditional way. Portfolio assessors are faculty subject matter experts who have likely taught the course being assessed and who determine whether credit can be awarded or not. In other words, this process is predicated on faculty judgement. The subjectivity and inconsistency only comes into play if the portfolio does not align with a course syllabus. Best practices dictate that if the learning is not in alignment, then credit is denied.

MYTH: Portfolio credits are awarded for students' work and life experience.

REALITY: College credit is only awarded for learning, not experience. Any portfolio that details work or life experience without linking that experience to *learning*—i.e., without being aligned with a course syllabus—will not be awarded college credits.

MYTH: Portfolio assessment is nothing but a stack of papers for which someone awards credit.

REALITY: Many erroneous visions of a student bringing in notebooks, certificates, and stacks of paper for an Admissions person to review and award credit have tainted faculty views on portfolio assessment. Students may use documents, such as certificates, letters of verification of learning, professional development transcripts, and more, to provide evidence of learning in the portfolio (see Chapter 2). However, the documentation must align with the student's description of her/his learning; and of course, the learning must also align with the syllabus.

Administrators must never assess portfolios. Only faculty subject matter experts who have received professional development in portfolio assessment can evaluate portfolios with integrity and rigor.

MYTH: Portfolio assessment will take students out of my classroom.

REALITY: It sounds counter-intuitive to disagree with this myth. Portfolio assessment students use their portfolios as way to earn credit without spending time in the classroom for subject matter that they already know. Yes, portfolio assessment students will bypass the classroom for those courses. However, research shows that PLA students are more likely to stay enrolled longer and take more courses over time than students who do not benefit from PLA (Klein-Collins 2010). Retaining students through to upper division courses or major courses that bring them closer to degree completion is what higher education is all about. On top of that, professors sometimes find students who are either bored with the content or who believe they have already "been there done that" can be contrary or dominate class discussions.

MYTH: Portfolio assessment students aren't prepared for subsequent courses in the series.

REALITY: Colleges and universities are only beginning to track student success post portfolio assessment. The research neither supports nor refutes this myth. However, because academic outcomes for students 25 years old or older who use PLA are far more positive, one may deduce that students who use PLA do not have any more difficulties with more advanced courses than those who took prerequisites in the classroom. After all, PLA students in the research graduate at twice the rate of non-PLA students (Klein-Collins 2010).

MYTH: Portfolio assessment is not allowed by my program accreditors.

REALITY: It cannot be assumed that just because an academic program has specialized accreditation (in addition to regional and/or national accreditation) that students are not allowed to participate in portfolio assessment. Increasingly, accreditors are recognizing the academic rigor associated with portfolio assessment. Always read the accrediting guidelines closely before denying students the opportunity to demonstrate their learning with portfolio assessment. Be sure to contact the accrediting agency if the guidelines do not address PLA or are unclear.

MYTH: Portfolio assessment is only for special adult degree completion programs.

REALITY: While many portfolio assessment programs historically have been rooted in adult degree completion programs, portfolio assessment today is much more mainstreamed. As student demographics have shifted, larger numbers of students enrolled in traditional baccalaureate programs are now able to access portfolio assessment. In fact, some states, such as Montana, Ohio, and Tennessee, to name a few, have been working with their systems to make all PLA methods acceptable at their public institutions.

Assessment in Portfolio Assessment

"Experience yields explicit knowledge only if reflected upon" (Fiddler, Marienau, and Whitaker 2006). In other words, without reflecting upon what we've learned from experience, there is no need for portfolio assessment. Indeed, experience is not learning. Portfolio assessors look for that kind of reflection in the student's writing; from a simple translation of the learning that has occurred from the experience to how that learning might be applied in a new and different situation to how that learning is leveraged to higher level knowledge and skills. A student must be able to articulate the learning as well as demonstrate that learning.

When experts describe experiential learning, they often rely upon David Kolb's *Cycle of Learning* (Colvin 2006). Kolb's model graphically shows how an individual can move from a "concrete experience" to thoughtful consideration of what has happened, why it happened, and how the outcome could be made better going forward through "reflection and observation." After reflection, "abstract conceptualization" begins during which the individual takes time to consider whether the outcome might be improved by doing something differently or whether the outcome might be achieved more efficiently by changing how something was done. This conceptualization leads the individual to try something new, or "actively experiment," to achieve the desired outcome. When a student is able to reflect upon experience in this way, the student will be successful in articulating learning for a portfolio assessment.

Kolb's Model of Experiential Learning

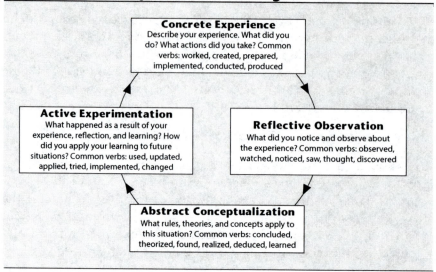

FIGURE 2. *Kolb's Model of Experiential Learning*

Kolb Examples Extracted from Actual Student Narrative

These excerpts from Jacqueline's portfolio help illustrate the value of Kolb's Cycle of Learning.

Learning objective as stated on the syllabus:

Gather and analyze information to make objective decisions based on factual data. Examine relevant strategies, issues, and considerations in purchasing. Exercise critical thinking skills. Evaluate brands and suppliers to meet organizational goals.

Jacqueline's narrative addressing the learning objective:

The ability to gather and present factual data is key in many aspects of the purchasing decision. The data gathered from usage, vendor selection, product selection, and price comparison ensures a smooth process to implementing a new product. For example, at my present employer, ABC Hotels[3], I purchased linen for 18 hotels. This included linen of different thread counts, sizes, etc.

> Note the recognition of critical thinking and reflective thought in this learning narrative, as well as how learning was derived from concrete experience.

One of my cost-saving goals for the year was to gather linen usage and cost information from the hotels. This data had many purposes. First, I wanted to determine if the usage and "spend" at the hotels was excessive or lacking. We compared one hotel's usage of linens to another with the same demographics (room sizes, pool). For instance, there were two hotels in similar locations that had a 30 percent difference in linen usage on a monthly basis. Because of the variance in usage, I met with the two hotels to isolate the factors driving the variance in usage. Some of the factors included the washing process, frequency of washings, and how long the linen was used before being discarded. This information helped us develop a more efficient usage process while at the same time ensuring

---

[3] Hotel name has been changed to protect student privacy.

the quality of the product being presented to the guest was consistent with the four-star rating of the ABC Hotel brand.

The second part of gathering the usage data enabled me to provide the information on the Request for Information (RFI) document to five vendors. After receiving the RFIs, I was able to narrow the selection to three vendors with the capabilities to service our hotels on a monthly basis based on usage. The RFI provided the data from the vendor that I used to determine that the supplier had the factory, warehouse, truck, and customer service capabilities that were needed to service 18 hotels monthly. With this data gathered and presented on a spreadsheet (**see Documentation D**), I met with our operational team at the corporate office to determine the specifications of linen we would implement as a brand standard for all the hotels. This enabled me to negotiate with leverage based on quantity because we would all use the same size, color, etc. Selecting a brand standard for all 18 hotels also ensures that the guest experience is consistent no matter which ABC Hotels they visit, thereby increasing guest loyalty.

> The student included Documentation D in the form of her actual work product: An ABC Hotel Spreadsheet detailing quantities of specific items and hotel locations as evidence to support her assertions.

Once the brand standard specification was selected, I put together a Request for Quote (RFQ) and sent it out to the three vendors. The usage and specification data provided to the vendors on the RFQ enabled me to compare pricing from all three vendors. Evaluating all the facts enabled me to select a vendor and negotiate a three-year contract.

Learning objective as stated on the syllabus:

Explain the management aspects of purchasing. Identify and explain purchasing systems and controls.

Jacqueline's narrative addressing the learning objective:

The management in purchasing has many facets; we must be aligned with the company's goals and objectives as well as keep our hands on the pulse of the multiple departments within the organization. This enables us to be part of the research and development of products and services utilized in various departments, such as IT, Marketing, and Sales. As purchasing managers, we possess highly developed skills and substantial managerial judgement to not only build and manage a world-class supply department, but to work closely with other areas within the organization (Fawcett 2000). Purchasing affects an organization's cost structure, lead times, time-to-market, flexibility, quality, and profitability (Raedels 2000).

> Note the citations used in this passage, as well as the specific concrete experience examples used to show the management aspects of purchasing.

My studies for the CPM [Certified Purchasing Manager] taught me that the purchasing manager needs to think strategically and broaden the perspective of supply management (Raedels 2000). This knowledge enabled me to expand my skills from an automated transaction to a larger scale of managing and implementing purchasing systems. Once I had developed my skills in strategic development, I applied the skill to everything that I was asked to purchase. Researching alternative solutions that were less costly with the same quality became one of my daily goals. I would then present the alternatives and supporting documentation for review and approval. For example, in 2013 there was a large renovation project at our flagship hotel in New York City, the ABC Hotel Regency. One of my tasks included researching and

> Note the active experimentation leading to abstract conceptualization and a new way to do a better, more efficient job.

locating an alternate fabric to a mohair fabric that was currently being used. The alternate fabric gave the same illusion as a mohair fabric, yet required less care and was therefore more practical for a guestroom. The cost savings presented was significant.

I learned the skill of value engineering many products. The key is to start the process early in the project. The Regency renovation enabled me to value engineer the light fixtures in the room, as well as the bathroom fixtures. Other approved products included lower costing alternative fabrics and a wallcovering re-designed at a lower cost. Given my experience with the Regency, I now currently review the designer's budgets to determine where the value engineering can be done prior to pricing new projects.

Describing the actual learning derived from experience is challenging for most students. Jacqueline's writing demonstrates how this link can be made through active experimentation and reflection.

In purchasing, systems and controls are in place to ensure that there are no unethical processes taking place within the transactions. The process of being transparent is common, as well as being prepared to be audited. At ABC Hotel, purchase orders (POs) are created for every transaction. The software system we are currently using is XYZ Software.[4] The purchase orders are contracts and are generated in order to protect the company from the vendor. Another control mechanism is all orders should have multiple bids (unless it's a single source product) with supporting documentation that can be reviewed at any time to support the awarding of the purchase order to a specific vendor. The main control in purchasing is not having both the invoices and checks processed in the same department. The accounting department receives a copy of the purchase order and can match the cost and items to the invoice once it arrives. This process eliminates any payoffs, purchasing of non-approved merchandise, and ensures everything and everyone is transparent to all departments.

---

[4] Software package name changed to keep content generic.

LET'S TAKE A LOOK

Anatomy of a Portfolio: Example #1—Jacqueline

Most institutions today use a "course match" process for assessment, meaning that a student's prior learning is mapped to the learning outcomes of an existing course. The first step in this process is for the student to find a course that aligns well with his or her learning. Our student, Jacqueline, searched the college catalog to find a course that aligned well with her experiential learning from her various positions in purchasing for hotels. Once Jacqueline identified this course, she was able to use its syllabus to find out what is expected of a student who takes the purchasing management course in a traditional manner.

Jacqueline's key goal for her portfolio was to align her learning with the course objectives or outcomes in a way that convinced the assessor that she has the same knowledge and skills as a student who completes and passes the course with a grade of "C" or better.

Excerpts from Jacqueline's portfolio (see Chapter 1) were used to show how Jacqueline learned in a cycle similar to Kolb's Theory. In this chapter, we will review Jacqueline's entire portfolio.

Jacqueline's portfolio is an excellent example of a high quality portfolio that scored very high on the portfolio rubric. It was awarded full credit.

Jacqueline followed the correct format for a portfolio:

1. **Course Information:** Including the course number, name, and number of credit hours for which a student is awarded upon passing the course.
2. **Learning Narrative Introduction:** Begins with an introduction to provide context for the assessment. Students generally provide some personal information, references to career progression, and academic goals as related to the portfolio.
3. **Learning Narrative:** Jacqueline uses the essay format using citations when applicable. She organizes the learning narrative by referencing each learning outcome, objective, competency, or topic. Notice how Jacqueline relates her experiences while teasing out the learning.
4. **References to Documentation:** Jacqueline shows the assessor how her various artifacts bring evidence to her experiential learning claims.
5. **Learning Narrative Conclusion:** Jacqueline presents her "final arguments for credit" for her portfolio.

6. **Documentation:** Jacqueline presents appropriate documentation in the form of work products, a resume showing her responsibilities as a purchasing manager, her *Certified Purchasing Manager* Certificate, and a letter of verification.
7. **References:** APA citations are specified in a References or Works Cited section.

The course for which Jacqueline seeks credit is BA-390 Purchasing Management, a 4.5 credit hour course.

Jacqueline's Portfolio

Please note: Key passages of Jacqueline's learning narrative are in bold-face type.

Course Description

This course provides the student with an understanding of the principles of purchasing materials and supply management. Emphasis is placed on the importance of these principles in the development of quality products and services and to profitable relations with suppliers, employees, and customers. Areas of study include quality, price, supplier selection, outsourcing, purchasing services, information flows, legal aspects, purchasing procedures and strategies, and international purchasing.

Jacqueline's Learning Narrative Introduction

My name is Jacqueline, I'm 49 years old and I live on Long Island, NY, with my husband of six years. I have a 32-year-old son. I am a purchasing manager for a well-known hotel company and a student part time. My husband and I are involved in our local parish and community. We teach fifth grade religious education on Saturday mornings during the school year, offer our services as readers, lead a weekly prayer group, and help supply the St. Vincent de Paul society.

This introduction provides just enough information for the reader to understand who Jacqueline is, her personal background as well as how she came to learn about Purchasing Management.

Jacqueline's experiences are briefly described to show her career progression and how her learning and skills became more sophisticated.

My learning experience started when I had my son at the age of 17. At a young age I learned and developed the skills of managing a family and household and developing my career in purchasing. I learned the skill of asking questions and to be persistent in stretching my learning skills. I have been in the corporate hospitality purchasing department of various large hotel chains for 28 years.

My experience in the purchasing industry began when I worked in the purchasing department as an assistant for three years; when the industry was still in its developing stages. Purchasing, as opposed to being a career, was more of an add-on clerical task given to the storeroom clerk, housekeeping department, or any other department that could pick up the phone and place an order for any item that the company needed. I developed my skill of placing daily food orders via phone and fax based on the needs and specification of the hotel chef. This task taught me the skill of obtaining various prices for the same item and comparing prices to determine the vendor that would be awarded the order based on pricing.

My next position, as a purchasing agent, with a larger chain of eight hotels continued for 10 years. I developed and honed the skills of purchasing for a group of hotels based in Manhattan. *This developed my skills of purchasing based not only on price but also my development of negotiating better pricing based on quality as well as leveraging the quantity of goods.*

I eventually became a purchasing manager for a group of seven hotels based in several regions of the country. My negotiation skills were enhanced because the properties were no longer located in the same area. *I researched and implemented several cost-saving strategies. For example, standardizing the brand of cleaning products that all the hotels would use and negotiating the price based on volume.* My skills in project management were developed in this position. For example, I managed the opening of a franchise hotel.

As the purchasing industry evolved, the Institute for Supply Management (ISM) developed the **Certified Purchasing Manager (CPM) designation**. I obtained my designation in 2010 (see Documentation A). I studied for the four module exam that taught me the various levels of supply management, including areas where I did not have much exposure, such as manufacturing purchasing and international buying. I realized that Handfield's definition was true: *"the purchasing functions are to support the needs of the organization in identifying, acquiring, accessing, positioning and managing the purchase of materials and service"*

Jacqueline references her designation as a Certified Purchasing Manager and includes the certificate in her "evidence" or documentation. She also demonstrates college-level writing by quoting experts in her field and using citations.

(Handfield 2008). **Over the last 28 years, since I began in the industry,** the position of purchasing manager has evolved into a critical position within the organization; it now ranks in the same level as top manager positions. The position was no longer a clerical task of processing papers but a position that would develop processes, procedures, and strategies that could enhance the company's bottom line.

My experience in the purchasing industry has helped me develop my learning and critical thinking skills and *continues to allow me cultivate these skills daily.*

The Body of the Learning Narrative

Like a lawyer laying out the case for the jury, the student needs to organize and present a compelling narrative and evidence for the portfolio assessor in a learning narrative. The student must organize the learning narrative in a logical manner, generally organized by the course's learning objectives or outcomes, point by point. If a syllabus is organized by topic, then the learning narrative will address each topic. In Jacqueline's case, the course syllabus was organized by learning objectives.

Jacqueline's learning narrative:

I will support my understanding and application of the purchasing process and skills based on my experience as a purchasing manager. I will present examples of the application, synthesis, and evaluation of the purchasing process and culture that has developed in the various companies I have been employed with.

I intend to demonstrate my knowledge, comprehension, and application in gathering and analyzing information to make objective decisions based on factual data as well as in identifying and explaining purchasing systems and controls.

Through my extensive years in purchasing, I have the details that support my ability to demonstrate the data being gathered, presented, and analyzed, which directly impacted the company's purchasing decisions based on the facts offered.

Objective #1: Gather and analyze information to make objective decisions based on factual data. Examine relevant strategies issues and considerations in purchasing. Exercise critical thinking skills. Evaluate brands and suppliers to meet organizational goals.

Jacqueline supports her assertion about the importance of data for decision making by describing a specific example, linking it to the challenge of reducing costs for linen, and describing the variables she needed to consider; thus, demonstrating critical thinking skills.

The ability to gather and present factual data is key in many aspects of the purchasing decision. The data gathered from usage, vendor selection, product selection, and price comparison ensures a smooth process to implementing a new product. For example, at my present employer, ABC Hotels, I purchased linen for 18 hotels. This included linen of different thread counts, sizes, etc. One of my cost-saving goals for the year was to gather linen usage and cost information from the hotels. This data had many purposes. First, I wanted to determine if the usage and spend at the hotels was excessive or lacking. We compared one hotel's usage of linens to another with the same demographics (room sizes, pool). For instance, there were two hotels in similar locations that had a 30 percent difference in linen usage on a monthly basis. Because of the variance in usage, I met with the two hotels to isolate the factors driving the variance in usage. Some of the factors included the washing process, frequency of washings, and how long the linen was used before being discarded.

Note how Jacqueline describes her experience and then goes on to explain what she learned—"a more efficient usage process [while ensuring quality consistent with the hotel brand]."

This information helped us develop a more efficient usage process while at the same time ensuring the quality of the product being presented to the guest was consistent with the four-star rating of the ABC Hotels brand. The second part of gathering the usage data enabled me to provide the information on the Request for Information (RFI) document to five vendors. After receiving the RFIs, I was able to narrow the selection to three vendors with the capabilities to service our hotels on a monthly basis based on usage. The RFI provided the data from the vendor that I used to determine that the supplier had the factory, warehouse, truck, and customer service capabilities that were needed to service 18 hotels monthly. *With this data gathered and presented on a spreadsheet (see Documentation D), I met with our operational team at the corporate office to determine the specifications of linen we would implement as a brand standard for all the hotels. This enabled me to negotiate with leverage based on quantity because we would all use the same size, color, etc.* Selecting a brand standard for all 18 hotels also ensures that the guest experience is consistent no matter which ABC Hotels they visit, thereby increasing guest loyalty. Once the brand standard specification was selected, I put together a Request for Quote (RFQ) and sent it out to the three vendors. The usage and specification data provided to the vendors on the RFQ enabled me to compare pricing from all three vendors. *Evaluating all the facts enabled me to select a vendor and negotiate a three year contract.*

Objective #2: Explain the scope of the purchasing activity and its evolution. Describe the structure and organization of purchasing.

While studying for my C.P.M exam, I learned that the purchasing function is to support the needs of the organization in identifying, acquiring, accessing, positioning, and managing the purchase of materials and services (Handfield 2008). I have studied, learned, and implemented the function in my day-to-day duties as a purchasing manager. The purchasing activities include the following steps (Fawcett 2000):

- Recognition of a need
- Description of a need
- Supplier selection and development
- Determination of price
- Purchasing at list price
- Competitive bidding
- Negotiation
- Preparation of purchase orders
- Follow-up and expediting
- Receipt and inspection
- Invoice clearance and supplier payment
- Performance monitoring and database management

These steps are the core steps in purchasing any commodity or service. I have used and followed these steps from buying food products, maintenance operational supplies (MRO), cleaning supplies, and furniture fixture & equipment (FF&E). Once the steps are followed in order, the success of accomplishing the organizational and department goal will be met. The steps that were developed elevated purchasing to a strategic function instead of just a clerical position.

Purchasing has evolved in the 28 years of my working experience, since my work experience began in the 1980s. I have seen the evolution of the position grow from clerical to a management position. I actually thought the evolution began in the 1980s, but I soon learned that the evolution and development of purchasing began much earlier than I realized. Changes in the supply environment have propelled purchasing's emergence as a valued contributor to organizational success (Fawcett 2000). The timeline below from The Supply Management Environment (Fawcett 2000) best describes the evolution of purchasing:

- Pre-World War II—Purchasing was viewed as a clerical function
- World War II—Purchasing receives increased emphasis
- 1950–early 1970s—Purchasing becomes a managerial function
- 1973–mid-1980s—Scarcity and inflation increase purchasing visibility
- 1985–1995—JIT partnering makes purchasing quasi-strategic
- 1995–Today—Outsourcing and SCM make purchasing strategic

Purchasing transformed with the infusion of better trained and more competent managers as well as the information technology expansion (Fawcett 2000).

In my years of experience I have viewed and been part of the purchasing department and the constant expansion and development of the purchasing department within an organization.

Objective #3: Explain the management aspects of purchasing. Identify and explain purchasing systems and controls.

The management in purchasing has many facets; we must be aligned with the company's goals and objectives as well as keep our hand on the pulse of the multiple departments within the organization. This enables us to be part of the research and development of products and services utilized in various departments, such as IT, Marketing, and Sales. As purchasing managers, we possess highly developed skills and substantial managerial judgement to not only build and manage a world-class supply department, but to work closely with other areas within the organization (Fawcett 2000). Purchasing affects an organization's cost structure, lead times, time-to-market, flexibility, quality, and profitability (Raedels 2000).

My studies for the CPM taught me that the purchasing manager needs to think strategically and broaden the perspective of supply management (Raedels 2000). **This knowledge enabled me to expand my skills from an automated transaction to a larger scale of managing and implementing purchasing systems.** Once I had developed my skills in strategic development, I applied the skill to everything that I was asked to purchase. *Researching alternative solutions that were less costly with the same quality became one of my daily goals.* I would then present the alternatives and supporting documentation for review and approval. For example, in 2013 there was a large renovation project at our flagship hotel in New York City, the ABC Hotels Regency. One of my tasks included researching and locating an alternate fabric to a mohair fabric that was currently being used. The alternate fabric gave the same illusion as a mohair fabric, yet required less care and was, therefore, more practical for a guestroom. The cost savings presented was significant.

I learned the skill of value engineering many products. The key is to start the process early in the project. The Regency renovation enabled me to value engineer the light fixtures in the room, as well as the bathroom fixtures. Other approved products included lower costing alternative fabrics and a wallcovering re-designed at a lower cost. Given my experience with the Regency, I now currently review the designer's budgets to determine *where the value engineering can be done prior to pricing new projects.*

In purchasing, systems and controls are in place to ensure that there are no unethical process taking place within the transactions. The process of being transparent is common, as well as being prepared to be audited. At ABC Hotels, purchase orders (POs) are created for every transaction. The software system we are currently using is XYZ Software. The purchase orders are contracts and are generated in order to protect the company from the vendor. Another control mechanism is all orders should have multiple bids (unless it's a single source product) with supporting documentation that can be reviewed at any time to support the awarding of the purchase order to a specific vendor.

The student succinctly describes purchasing systems and controls as per Objective #3.

The main control in purchasing is not having both the invoices and checks processed in the same department. The accounting department receives a copy of the purchase order and can match the cost and items to the invoice once it arrives. This process eliminates any payoffs, purchasing of non-approved merchandise, and ensures everything and everyone is transparent to all departments.

Objective #4: Summarize the key purchasing variables of quality, quantity, time, source, price, and negotiation.

When developing a Request for Pricing or Quote (RFP or RFQ), the specification is provided to the vendor based on quantity and delivery time frame. Providing this information will generate the price from the vendor that can be reviewed and negotiated. It is important to obtain all this information prior to sending the RFP to the vendors; it ensures that the pricing received from all the vendors can be compared and negotiated because the same information was used to determine price by all the vendors.

Throughout my career, I learned that negotiation of pricing is not the only variable that is negotiable. Timing, freight, packaging, and quantities are also negotiating factors.

Everything is negotiable. During the Regency renovation project, freight became an issue when staying under budget. It became a negotiating tool when selecting a vendor.

Another helpful tool in purchasing is a GANTT chart. I utilized this chart while working with furniture suppliers for the Regency renovation project (see Documentation E—GANTT Chart: The Regency Project). The tool maintained the schedule and communicated the delivery dates to the vendors and the general contractor.

> More evidence is provided by including the GANTT chart.

Objective #5: Gather and analyze data (compare variables) which affect a person's and an organization's purchasing decisions and make purchasing recommendations based on the information.

When implementing a purchasing strategy, the information gathered and presented will help determine if the strategy will be approved or rejected. The bottom line is if the cost savings for the organization (either in time or money) cannot be supported, the strategy will not be approved and further research will need to be performed.

For example, I researched and presented a Group Purchasing Organization (GPO) buying program that leveraged our buying power for 18 hotels. The information presented assisted upper management in approving the strategy implementation based on the cost savings and standardization of various products. It was determined that various categories could be negotiated at the same time when dealing with a GPO. The biggest category was food buying for all the hotels. We zoned in on the category of meats, dairy, and produce. Presenting the ability to work with one major food supplier, Sysco, under the umbrella of the GPO enabled the hotels to see a 15 percent reduction in food cost within the first year of implementation. At that time, bringing the savings of food cost to upper management opened the door for approvals of several other categories to be researched and the GPO to be utilized in other areas of the hotel.

The concept of being transparent with a vendor and partnering has become a valuable tool in my purchasing success. I have established multiple partnerships with vendors. Two examples are the linen vendor and the GPO vendor. These partnerships were developed and maintained to bring continuous savings to the company. The concept of using a vendor once is antiquated. **Forming and establishing partnerships and long-term relationships with vendors eliminates the constant need for research to procure new vendors.**

Objective #6: Evaluate the importance of ethical and social responsibility in purchasing and organizational decision-making. Explain how the environment affects purchasing decision-making. Assess the importance of purchasing activities and applications, dealing with processes associated with buying in particular markets.

When forming a partnership with a vendor, researching the company is an important step. We do not want to partner with companies that hire young children in the factories or who do not pay a fair wage. *The location of the factory and the culture of the company that we are partnering with speaks to our ethical and social responsibility. We need to ensure that the company's mission is in line with our company's mission.* During a recent visit to a furniture vendor, I traveled to inspect a factory within the United States and to meet the people working for the company. Because companies also have their factories overseas, researching the company and their ethics and social responsibility became a critical step in evaluating a company with which to form a partnership. Vendors are now considered partners and not just a one-time source. I learned how to evaluate vendors by performing preliminary surveys, checking financials, and visiting the factories. These tools enable us to get a transparent view of the company and their ability to service our organization.

Conclusion

The conclusion of Jacqueline's learning narrative reinforces her case for credit.

My daily activities at work support my competency in the course objectives. **I have learned** and been a part of the evolution of the purchasing manager position. It has been both rewarding and challenging. Obtaining my CPM has enabled me to expand my knowledge from day-to-day activities to bringing it up a notch to supply management level. I have been privileged to work for corporations that have enabled me to put into effect cost-saving strategies that have impacted the company's bottom line. *I plan to continue learning* new concepts in purchasing so I can continue to maintain and improve my professional competence and strive to maintain and improve the competence of my colleagues, which will enable us to all to be an asset to our company. I will continue to take courses through work to understand the changes to the systems and environment. *The hopeful success of this narrative will support my continuous goal of completing my Bachelor degree and, therefore, open the door for my pursuit of an MBA.*

Jacqueline's learning narrative, as in all portfolio learning narratives, included a References section.

Documentation

Documentation provides additional authenticity to the student's portfolio. Documentation generally includes various artifacts that support the student's assertions. Examples of documentation may include:

- ✓ Certificates and licenses
- ✓ Professional development transcripts
- ✓ Letters of verification from an expert or employer attesting to specific learning outcomes, objectives, or competencies referenced in the learning narrative
- ✓ PowerPoint presentations
- ✓ Resume (Note: the resume is only used to document one's experience)
- ✓ Work products, such as spread sheets, strategic plans, newsletters, reports, and websites
- ✓ Audio or video recordings of the student performing specific tasks, such as making a speech or performing a specific skill

Jacqueline's documentation listed and described below provides good evidence that what she said she knew and could do was true.

Jacqueline's documentation/artifacts:

Documentation A—CPM Certificate

Jacqueline was able to provide a color copy/image of her Certified Purchasing Manager award from the Institute for Supply Management. The certificate includes a raised gold seal, the date of the award, and signatures. The CPM designation is a highly respected credential in purchasing management. It serves as an excellent evidential artifact for her learning narrative.

Documentation B—Resume

Jacqueline's resume shows her career progression in the purchasing management field from 1990 to today. It is further evidence of her longevity in the field and provides specific examples of her work. Strong resumes that tie directly to the learning narrative are helpful evidence. Resumes are not in and of themselves evidence of learning; rather, they can support the student's learning claim by providing personal context, as Jacqueline did in her introduction to the learning narrative.

Documentation C—Letter of Verification

Jacqueline's letter of verification provides third party testimony to her skills as a purchasing manager. Notice how specific the letter is in referencing her experience and skills. It reinforces the learning narrative in several ways:

1. It shows the number of years Jacqueline has been working in the field honing her skills and learning about purchasing management.
2. It references specific projects that align with the learning narrative.
3. It shows the scope of her experience as well as her critical thinking skills developed as a result of her experiences.
4. It references her ongoing professional development.

ABC Hotels

(Company Letterhead)

July 17, 2015

Dear Portfolio Evaluator:

This letter confirms that Jacqueline has been employed at ABC Hotels on a full-time basis since 2004 as a Purchasing Manager. Jacqueline is one of my direct reports and has worked on many capital projects from inception to completion.

During her employment, Jacqueline has demonstrated strong purchasing skills in various settings. Her ability to complete projects has demonstrated her skills in areas such as data gathering, negotiations, presentation, and value engineering. Her professional skills as well as her ability to be a team player are highlighted with her interaction with our vendors as well as our customers, i.e., the hotels. She has developed numerous cost-saving strategies that have been implemented throughout our 23 hotel portfolio.

For example, during the renovation of the ABC Regency Hotel, our flagship property, she demonstrated her ability to implement critical thinking to resolve multiple challenges. Her skills in coordinating vendor deliveries to the hotel resulted in maintaining the project schedule. Jacqueline utilized her financial discipline in maintaining and reconciling the multi-million dollar budget for the furniture, fixtures, and equipment (FF&E) project.

Jacqueline presents concise analytical data in order to assist me in making timely and financially sensitive decisions. One of her strengths is her ability to manage and keep the ever changing procurement process moving in the right direction without compromising our quality standards and our demanding time frames.

Jacqueline continues to keep herself abreast of purchasing and supply management skills by attending seminars and maintaining her interaction with the Institute of Supply Management. She has performed well above average in her purchasing skills. Her performance evaluation is consistently ranked high (4.5 out of a possible 5).

I wish Jacqueline the best in her educational endeavors. Please feel free to contact me for more information.

Sincerely,

V.P. Signature Here

Vice President, Facilities

Documentation D—Analysis Worksheet—ABC Hotels 23 Hotel Linen Usage and Spend

As further evidence, Jacqueline included a work product spreadsheet detailing purchase order numbers, quantities, and order dates organized by hotel location. The linen usage and spend spreadsheet indicates the level of detail, documentation, and organization required for Jacqueline's job. Spreadsheet linen items include quantities and pricing for hand/face towels, bath sheets, bath towels, pool towels, wash cloths, sheets by sizes, pillow cases by sizes, and various bath rugs by sizes.

Documentation E—GANTT Chart—The ABC Regency Project

The Gantt chart provides evidence of Jacqueline's responsibilities as a purchasing manager during a major hotel renovation. The chart details 26 different tasks associated with the project, including start and end dates (duration of the various tasks). It also includes the deadlines for request of proposals and purchase orders.

The Assessment

The faculty subject matter expert who assessed Jacqueline's portfolio used a rubric to ensure the following was achieved with the portfolio:

- Learning objectives were each addressed thoroughly and convincingly demonstrating a level of mastery for all course outcomes
- The student is able to differentiate between learning and experience
- The student references how learning has been transferred to other environments
- The student demonstrates reflective and critical thinking
- The student is able to cite broader theoretical or conceptual links related to the learning
- The student demonstrates college-level writing (strong thesis statements, arguments which follow a logical order, and focused)
- The student's documentation is authentic and supports the learning narrative

Jacqueline was awarded 4.5 credit hours for **BA-390 Purchasing Management**.

3 LEARNING OUTCOMES, COMPETENCIES, AND CREDIT

The course syllabus provides critical information for the student's successful development of a learning portfolio. Essentially, it is the road map for the learning narrative. First, the course description provides the student with a general overview of course content to determine if the student's learning might align with the course. Here is an example of a course description for the three-credit-hour course BBM320 Business Communication:

> This course is a detailed study and application of various types of oral and written communication used in business. Included are technologies that enhance communication effectiveness, international considerations, presentation and interviewing skills, and written forms of communication, such as memos, procedures, resumes, and formal reports. Students' writing skills are evaluated through a written assignment during the first class.

The course description provides sufficient information for the student to determine whether or not he or she is familiar with the course topics. Without further information, the student would need to develop a portfolio with very little information beyond addressing the four topics, all at the college level.

If the student obtains a syllabus for the Business Communication course, then the student is able to see the required textbooks, materials, and assignments for the course. Most importantly, though, the student needs to be able to find the learning outcomes and/or competencies for the course to prepare a top-notch portfolio. Clearly articulated learning outcomes or competencies are at the heart of every successful portfolio. Students must demonstrate what they know and can do; but without specific outcomes or competencies, the demonstration can stray off course or worse, miss the target altogether. Course transparency not only articulates course objectives but also states what students should be able to "do" as a result of successfully completing a course. The more specific, the better for students seeking credit through portfolios.

Even with the learning outcomes defined, if they are vague or ambiguous, the student will have more difficulty aligning learning as well as trouble focusing the learning narrative. Poorly defined outcomes do not provide enough detail to result in a portfolio that is sufficient to earn credit. When outcomes and competencies are clear, the student can much more easily determine if, in fact, she has actually mastered the content in a manner consistent with the outcomes. Here is an example of clear learning outcomes for a BBM320 Business Communication course:

Learning Outcomes and Competencies

Example

GOAL A—Prepare and deliver clear, concise, complete, and correct oral and written business communications.

Learning Outcomes: *The student will...*

Learning outcomes or competencies clearly identify what students must know and be able to do.

A-1—Demonstrate effective writing skills, including proper grammar and punctuation.

A-2—Identify the important steps involved in prewriting and revising during the writing process.

A-3—Demonstrate effective oral presentation skills, including keeping the audience's attention, nonverbal communication, and persuasion of point of view.

GOAL B— Explain the purpose of a variety of business communications.

Learning Outcomes: *The student will...*

B-1—Identify what form of business communications should be used in the appropriate business situation.

B-2—Differentiate the writing style used according to the form of communication.

B-3—Develop a persuasive formal business report.

B-4—Define the proper use of e-mail within the business environment.

B-5—Apply the written and oral concepts involved in developing job materials and successful interviewing.

B-6—Discuss the importance of good communication skills to project management.

GOAL C—Investigate research strategies for gathering information in a formal report.

Learning Outcomes: *The student will...*

C-1—Identify primary resources in the business environment.

C-2—Identify secondary resources in the business environment.

C-3—Differentiate the various databases used for business communications.

C-4—Identify the limitations associated with various Internet sources.

C-5—Apply the concepts of APA writing style to the formal business report.

GOAL D—Apply contemporary information technologies while creating a variety of business communications.

Learning Outcomes: *The student will...*

D-1—Present a PowerPoint demonstration of the formal business report.

D-2—Identify the best type of graphics for use with the appropriate business communication.

GOAL E—Demonstrate awareness of international business protocol.

Learning Outcomes: *The student will...*

E-1—Identify various ethical differences in the global business environment.

E-2—Discuss cultural issues as they relate to business communications.

GOAL F—Describe the importance of good listening skills in the business environment.

Learning Outcomes: *The student will...*

F-1—Identify the steps involved in active listening.

F-2—Explain the factors associated with listening to non-native speakers in the workplace.

Not all college and university syllabi have such explicit outcomes listed. When the outcomes are not clear, students will need to be more resourceful in finding out what is expected of a student who completes the course with a "C" grade or above. Students can generally check out the textbooks that are listed on the syllabus to gain insight to the outcomes of the course. Once this is accomplished, the student may be able to have a conversation with a faculty member who teaches the course to determine if the student is on track.

Student Portfolio Example #2—Christine

BBM320—Business Communication Portfolio Learning Narrative

Introduction

My name is Christine Fenimore Kubik.[5] I am 45 years old and live in Middletown, Delaware, with my two children. I am attending a university to obtain my BS in Organizational Management.

Currently, I am the Employer Support Specialist assigned to the Delaware National Guard. I serve extensively in the community and am always known for helping others. I have a high work ethic, exceptional organization skills, and am very driven which has earned me the respect of others. I am currently a Founding Board Member of the First State Military Academy, a new JROTC charter high school in my local area. Giving back and serving others has been a lifelong trait that has led me into a rewarding career, and challenged me in numerous volunteer roles.

> The student provides a good overview of who she is as well as an overview of her vast experience in business communication. This sets the context for the assessment.

Throughout my 20+ year professional career (see Document A: Resume Christine Kubik), I have managed and spearheaded successful marketing and business development programs, where communication has been critical to their achievement. I have originated and led organizational and administrative management initiatives as well as delivered exceptional public relations and networking. **I have prepared, coordinated, and delivered speeches, presentations, and all formats of written and electronic information materials. At a higher level, I have analyzed, evaluated, implemented, and written new procedures and processes for business operations.** I have developed and written comprehensive business operation plans. I have created and delivered briefings to leadership on same as well as reporting on business growth and status. I continue to routinely create all levels of written format, including letters, e-mails, and

---

[5] This portfolio's author, Christine Fenimore Kubik, gave permission to use her portfolio for this book.

reports. I was recently responsible for the development of a nationwide performance metrics and narrative report for each team member to use to present monthly to upper level leadership.

In this essay, I will validate my experiential learning to meet the requirements and objectives of the course "BBM320: *Business Communications*." This course is a detailed study and application of various types of oral and written communication used in business. Included are technologies that enhance communication effectiveness, international considerations, presentation and interviewing skills, and written forms of communication, such as memos, procedures, resumes, and formal reports.

> This section is very much about her experiences, as opposed to what she has learned from the experience. The assessor will keep a keen eye out for how the student will describe her learning beyond these experiences. However, because the learning outcomes are about "outputs" (the delivery of different forms of communication), the student is still on the right track with this section.

GOAL A: *Prepare and deliver clear, concise, complete, and correct oral and written business communications.*

Whether it was my professional experience or volunteerism, I have always sourced my talent to be an effective author of business correspondence, from e-mails to letters to invitations to thank you note cards. I consistently communicate with my targeted audience and customers (see Document B: ***Employer Breakfast with the General*** invitation, e-mail, and thank you). Recently I initiated a new event for employers of our soldiers and airmen in the Delaware National Guard to be invited to a breakfast event with our Adjutant General. The communications on the event needed to entice attendance, while keeping with protocol of our host, a two-star high ranking officer. To win over an hour of an attendee's time can sometimes be a challenge, especially when the guest lists includes CEOs and presidents and business leaders. I needed to convey that their time is valued. With a combination of concise directions and the working relationship with these employers, we have been at maximum attendance for each event, and all deemed successful in offering appreciation for our civilian employers.

During these events, like many others, there is an oral presentation piece shared by a few. Writing the agenda and staying on track is also an important component. Typically, I am always the facilitator of these types of gatherings, which requires me to always address the group. In this instance, I am carrying the group conversation at a high level and making sure our guest speakers are timely too. The program has to run smoothly in order for the attendees to feel the hour was well spent (see Document C: Letters of Verification—to show I can successfully prepare and deliver clear, concise, complete, and correct oral and written business communications).

While in my tenure at XYZ Fitness, Inc. and ABC's Famous Motorcycles[6], I was called up to work on upgrading and, at times, authoring various written policies and standard operating procedures (SOPs) for the benefit of the organization. Working with other department heads and employees was key in order to capture the flow of procedures. In my role at XYZ Fitness, our operations were dropping and training was depleted. I was hired and immediately tasked to underwrite SOPs for the business, as none had existed previously. The business suffered from quick growth, and did not develop the business simultaneously in key areas. SOPs ensured a cohesive teamwork between all departments. They were also meant to allow other departments to understand the importance of each other. The procedures were done in detail and developed from my shadowing employees at all levels, who actually performed the work. As with any written work, they started out in draft and went through many reviews and revisions. I sought the help of those I shadowed and department heads to ensure the procedures were accurate and a direct reflection of the systems and processes.

---

[6] Names changed to make content generic.

It is funny for me to think back to an "Oral Presentation" class I took in college in 1989. My instructor had so much faith in me that by the end of the class I would not be sweating bullets, white-knuckled to the podium, and delivering in a crackled voice. Many who know me today never believe that story because I prepare, create, and deliver briefings like it's second nature. **But over the years, I had to teach myself and set my own standards to improve.** I coached myself and built up my own confidence level, in small steps. I knew I was capable and just needed to set up realistic expectations of myself. I began by running meetings in small group settings, advanced to addressing small groups, growing to larger, to now today; I will conduct briefings to over 1,000 at one time. **One key support to my learning was my ability to create PowerPoint slides to not only enhance delivery and reinforce the message and presentation, but also to help guide me and keep me on track, so that my oral piece was clear and to the point.** I also continue this practice today, by using my audience's feedback. In my current role, I give briefings to soldiers and airmen on their civilian employment job protections. As the audience would ask questions in the briefings, I tended to go back and update my slides to reflect and/or address those questions, or trends. Also, **I pay attention to my audience and observe what information grabs their attention, what parts they ask questions on, etc. and make any revisions based on that.**

Here the student shows evidence of reflection.

GOAL B: *Explain the purpose of a variety of business communications.*

During the year 2012 when deployments were higher, it became abundantly evident that there was a huge need to start addressing issues of unemployment amongst veterans. That said, my current role and responsibilities at the Guard shifted to be able to address and offer employment assistance to those who were job seeking. As a way to educate myself, I reached out to the Department of Labor for the review of the Delaware Joblink network and their staff, as well as various Department of Defense websites, such as American Jobs for America's Heroes and Veterans Job Bank. One task that became a primary duty and need amongst those I served was resume building (see Document D: 3 Sample Resumes, personal information removed). I think one of the most important forms of communication representing our professional and education backgrounds is a resume. I assisted our soldiers and airmen in all facets of their employment, which includes interviewing tips and coaching, job searching, and resume development. It is key to make sure the resume document is concise, accurate, no typos or grammar mistakes or misspellings, and effectively represents the skills one brings to the job applied for. **Many times our Guard member experiences a greater challenge, by putting in writing and translating their military skills to the civilian equivalent. I assist them in this process, and taught myself how best to approach the translation and developed resources that I found most helpful.** It is important that they be sure the reviewer understands the skill sets that qualify them for the job, and that they are represented on the resume, in order to be selected to interview. A resume is a first impression. I have written over 200 resumes in the last year. I am constantly making sure I am providing top-notch service and offering the latest trends gathered from HR professionals.

Christine delivers compelling evidence of the power of doing research to understand one's audience and to address perceived objections in a thoughtful, strategic manner.

I will never forget the most intense presentation I had to offer over the course of my career. It was a presentation during my time at ABC's Famous Motorcycles in 2006. There were many instances, but this one in particular was for a public workshop to a town in Connecticut, where we wanted to build a new ABC's Motorcycle dealership. And we were received by the community with an emphatic "not my town—go away" message. I became tasked by our Owner/Dealer to sway their hearts and minds, and get them to a supportive place. These audiences, whether speaking to a small group or one or large audience, were my most intense audiences. Every correspondence, invitation, letter, and slide show presentation was strategic and set to develop and persuade the local community to "welcome" us and embrace our new presence in an area dominated by elderly citizens and very serene nature. In order to educate myself to tackle the best approach, I researched the geographic area, neighborhood, people, other businesses, town events, etc. I prepared a persuasive slide show and presentation that would change the minds of "future neighbors" to our proposed ABC's Famous Motorcycles dealership (see Document E: Slide Show, Public Workshop). In order to win the audience over, the presentation had to contradict all the stereotypical comments being made about ABC's Motorcycles. I realized it was an uphill battle, and made sure to draw attention to the ABC's Motorcycle customer who was of like-demographics, and speak to all the charitable giving we offered in our other local communities. **Face-to-face networking and communicating in-person was key to our success.**

I will always remember this presentation, as it was the most intense of my career. But it has always reminded me to be sure I am looking at the "full picture" when giving presentations.

GOAL C: Investigate research strategies for gathering information in a formal report.

Here the student is directly addressing each of the goals A, B, C, and D, as well as citing an external source using APA style.

From the experience to build our ABC's Motorcycle dealership, it was very important to gather and know the audience. While there was a team of department heads involved in the project, my part was to know the area's demographics and make relationships and network, being the spokesperson. Looking at the big picture in all my marketing positions, I was responsible to write, implement, and follow an annual marketing business plan. Having a good, solid plan allows for efficient execution. In order to drive customers to any business, you must be able to send messages to them through various forms of communications and advertisement that are meant to raise brand awareness and support the common goal, likely sales/revenue (see Document F: MFHD Marketing Business Plan). "Whether you market your business online, in person or through traditional advertising, communication is key to brand awareness. Be responsive. A big part of marketing is being available to your target audience and following up when necessary. If you market your business through social media outlets—including Twitter, Facebook and blogging—watch for and respond to comments, questions and especially complaints. And when you are contacted as a result of offline marketing activities, respond quickly and professionally. And, write well. You can't successfully promote your business if your marketing copy is not clear, concise and action-provoking" (Noupe Editorial Team 2010, p. 1).

The student addresses B-3 directly. She also demonstrates Kolb's Theory of Learning by adapting what she does as she goes to get the desired result, or learning from her experience.

Six years ago, when I started my current position, I was hired specifically for my forte to bring direction, professionalism, and communication to the organization. I developed a Business Plan for the organization to increase volunteerism and increase reaching the goals. I developed and standardized all communications, whether written or oral presentations, so that we always delivered the same message (see Document G: DE ESGR Business Plan FY10, sample letters.)

Also for my peers, we found ourselves lost without training opportunities. I was tasked by my company to develop and implement training for all new personnel, who were hired into my same position across the nation. I was asked to pull a group of my peers together and formulate a training subcommittee that would together provide the deliverables. The training plan was comprehensive of state needs, meanwhile supportive of a national strategic plan that we all could buy-into and follow. As a result, we became the first National Guard program to have an abundance of metrics and performance reports available. In developing the report, I walked through our job duties one by one and pulled out those duties that could be quantified and show productivity to the customer in the monthly report. **Quantifying our performance was key to the success of the report, and stability and security of the program, especially during budget cuts**. I held various meetings with all key stakeholders and researched what other programs were doing to report their productivity. As part of the training, I wrote best practices that could be easily implemented by a new staff member, like form letters to employers, e-mails to service members, job posting e-mails, and the like. This enabled them to hit the ground running, and not have to re-invent the wheel of tools that were readily available. I researched and found that our own company had a portal available, as well as a storage database, that I had access to and could use to be able to share files with my peers nationwide. **I noticed** after several months of implementation, while the metrics were critical to reporting, a narrative section needed to provide the full picture. The metrics alone were not enough. *So I developed* and initiated a standard format that could be customized with each state's information and reporting that month (see Document H: DENG FY14 Metrics Report and Narrative). The report is ever changing. I learned to listen to superiors each month on submission and make sure tweaks were made along the way to continue delivering a quality report product.

GOAL D: Apply contemporary information technologies while creating a variety of business communications.

In the absence of annual and quarterly conferences in person, as well as the mere fact that our Guard employer support team was spread across the nation, we became dependent on system applications and strategic uses of information technology to accomplish our job duties, as well as correspond with each other. Our key stakeholders and customers were the service members, and employers—and reaching them could sometimes prove challenging.

Because of the success in addressing unemployment issues with the Guard, and setting and following a successful master plan to reduce unemployment amongst military members, the Guard was asked, and I was assigned, to work with the Delaware Workforce Investment Board (DWIB) to assist overall veteran unemployment in our state. Two years ago, the Board adopted a goal in their strategic plan to reduce veteran unemployment in the state to below the general population rate. The plan was built on education and raising awareness to employers of the value to hire the talent, skill, and discipline any uniformed member brings to the workforce. A consistent message was built, and the veteran subcommittee of the DWIB set out in their mission. The subcommittee members worked for different agencies and organizations, but we all worked together to stay consistent in the message we delivered. Slide show presentations were developed, so we were all educating the audience on the same information (see Document I: Hiring Veterans Makes Good Business Sense). Information in the Department of Labor database and web resources, as well as the Delaware National Guard's, were reflective of the same assistance. Recently, I prepared a slide show presentation for the Delaware Workforce Investment Board on veteran employment to ask that they continue to keep the focus on reducing vet unemployment as a priority for the group, as they renewed their Strategic Plan. Over the last two years the goal has been in place, it was easily observed by the stats in the presentation the group has accomplished milestones towards the goal, and its reduction (see Document J: DWIB Strategic Planning Session). **A key success over the last two years was learning the importance of partnering with other agencies, documenting progress along the way, and being better informed of resources and existing programs, as to avoid duplicity.**

And just like any young adult, which the 18–24 year old is a large target audience for me on unemployment, you have to be where they are. Most young adults are on social media, and if you are not there too, you won't reach them through the communication method that they have grown to rely on, and be engorged with. "Most likely you write and create digital documents with computers and other Internet-enabled electronic devices in today's networked environment without thinking much about the technology enabling you to do all this. Information technology has changed how we work, play, and communicate in distinct ways. It has never been easier to access and share information via digital media from a vast network of sources and to distribute it nearly instantly and to widespread audiences. What hasn't changed is that communication skills need time and effort to develop" (Guffey 2014, p. 6). Becoming familiar with modern communication technology can help you be successful on the job. **I have had great success through social media advertisement in reaching our young soldiers and airmen through messages on Facebook, Twitter, and the like.** As I looked around the room at a recent event I attended for their holiday celebrations, most of the soldiers either had a smartphone in their hand, or set in the place setting in front of them. Getting focused on our target age group, 18–24 year olds, all members of the veteran subcommittee of the DWIB have spent time educating ourselves on social media, hashtags, keywords, etc., to be able to be more effective in this communication venue to reach our target audience.

GOAL E: Demonstrate awareness of international business protocol.

It's a globalizing world. I did not have much experience in this section goal of the course, so I researched to find more and develop a better understanding. "When considering starting a small business, it may not occur to you to consider exporting your product. However, according to the Small Business Association, 96 percent of the world's potential customers live outside of the United States" (US Small Business Administration 2010, p. 1). "The international market is lucrative, though the legal environment for operating in that forum is different from that for a business that operates exclusively within the borders of the United States. For this reason, it is important to be familiar with some of the basic concepts of doing business in the global economy. You may be acquainted with challenges faced by US businesses and workers when considering the questions associated with this new business environment. When we shop for food, computers, clothing, pet food, automobiles, or just about anything produced for the global market, we might very well purchase a final product from a different country, or a product composed of components or labor from many different parts of the world. Economists tell us that this represents the most efficient method of production and labor. After all, if a business can pay $1 per hour to a worker overseas, why would it choose instead to pay $12 per hour to a US worker?" (Schmitz 2012, p. 1).

I would anticipate that in doing business in the global economy, you would have to understand various protocols, customs, and practices of any country you were doing business with. If you are a business owner who must travel abroad, when you are visiting you must be schooled on culture etiquette and communications, as not to offend your customers. You need to know how to dress, how to say hello, and who to address first, or not at all. You will need to take into consideration how to host any event or reception, as well as business meetings. It may be appropriate, or even expected, to offer gifts in certain countries and cultures. This would be very similar to even within our own country, how Americans observe various religious observations during the month of December; many times it is not practical for businesses to communicate "Merry Christmas" vs. "Seasons' Greetings" or "Happy Holidays."

GOAL F: Describe the importance of good listening skills in the business environment.

Daily, I answer questions as they arise to a uniformed member's civilian job protections and an employer's obligation to the Uniformed Services Employment and Re-employment Rights Act (USERRA) law. The key to any mediation is listening carefully to parties, drawing on the facts, and providing construction feedback in hopes of a resolution without further escalation. Providing the wrong info back can and will affect an individual's income and employment. I have learned to listen for key elements and facts. As I listen, I have made it a habit to write things down that are the key elements and important facts as they relate to a potential law violation. I always reiterate and summarize to all parties to ensure we stay on the same page.

As mentioned earlier in the essay, a large part of my current position is education and outreach. To do this, I conduct many presentations and briefings on civilian job protections and obligations to USERRA law and employment assistance. I always make sure to listen to the audience, ask questions in my briefings, and update my slides to reflect and/or address those questions, or trends. I try to be sure to listen to my audience and observe what information grabs their attention, what parts they ask questions on, etc. and make any revisions based on that. We throw so much information at them, I try to make sure I am an interactive speaker, listen to comments being made, and do my best to spontaneously provide relevant information to the subject we are discussing.

Conclusion

Developed over the last 20 years of my professional marketing and public relations career, effective business communication has been a skilled talent and integral part of my successful career. I would not have enjoyed it without the ability to efficiently and effectively produce dynamic and persuasive communications, oral or written. Whether, it was a simple letter, an oral presentation, or message on social media, business communication is present and an important part of raising any brand awareness in any business. I have demonstrated in my career my learning over the years to improve my skills and use of effective writing skills. I have tremendously improved my ability to deliver speeches and effective oral presentation skills, including keeping the audience's attention, and even a persuasion of point of view. It has always been critical for me to understand the project at hand, and deliver in the appropriate business situation. I have learned to stay on top of the latest technologies used for business communications. Over and over again, I am called upon to create and deliver a PowerPoint presentation or create business reports. In the new age of social media, I have learned that there will always be a new form of communication tool to use to get your message to your target audience. However, being clear, concise, and communicating effectively is essential. Staying on top of technology is important as there is always something new to be learned. Pursuing a degree in Organizational Management has afforded me the learning opportunity to fill in gaps, where my professional career might not cross. I feel I have demonstrated throughout the previous pages how my experience, knowledge, learning, and understanding of the core principles of business communication meet the course objectives. I hope that you will see this as well and approve my petition for my Business Communication (BBM320) portfolio.

> The student has written an effective conclusion, adding closing arguments for the case for credit.

References

Guffey, M. 2014. *Business communication: Process and product* 8th ed.. Stamford, CT: Guffey and Loewy.

Noupe Editorial Team. 2010. *12 secrets of effective business communication.* Retrieved from www.noupe.com

Schmitz, A. 2012. *Business and the legal and ethical environment* 1st ed. Retrieved from http://2012books.lardbucket.org/books/business-and-the-legal-and-ethical-environment/s16-business-in-the-global-legal-e.html

US Small Business Administration. 2010. *Take your business global.* Retrieved from www.sba.gov

Christine's Documentation

In addition to the letter of verification below, the student included the following documents in support of her case for credit:

- Student's Resume
- Employer Breakfast with the general invitation, e-mail, and thank you communications
- Three sample resumes
- The slide show for the Public Workshop
- Accountability Business Plan
- ESGR Business Plan FY12 including sample letters and newsletters
- Hiring Veterans Makes Sense communication
- Strategic Planning Session documents

Military Affairs Letterhead

March 5, 2015

To Whom It May Concern:

As Ms. Kubik's onsite supervisor, please accept the following verification of her knowledge, skills, and abilities performed in her current position. She has been employed in the same position for almost 7 years.

She has given countless oral presentations, unit briefings, pre-mobilization and demobilization Yellow Ribbon Reintegration Briefings, and the like to hundreds of Guard members and families. At times, she is addressing a unit/group anywhere between 25–300 uniformed personnel, or employers of our Guard members.

Ms. Kubik educates military members and their employers on issues surrounding civilian employment, to include a service member's job protections and responsibilities under the Uniformed Services Employment and Reemployment Rights Act (USERRA), as well as employment assistance services available through her office. She also provides families with information on their military leave entitlements under Family Medical Leave Act (FMLA) surrounding a qualified family members' deployment. Ms. Kubik is responsible for maintaining employer relations and coordinating.

Ms. Kubik performs her duties by delivering comprehensive briefings through her creation of informative slides, and delivering information in a thorough, concise format. Her oral presentation skills show years of experience that provide for a polished professional presence in her presentations. It is without reservation that I verify Ms. Kubik's abilities in the public speaking arena.

I am available for any questions pertaining to this memo.

Sincerely,

Signature Here

Colonel

Delaware Army National Guard

The Assessor's Evaluation

In reviewing Christine's portfolio, it is always important to remember that the portfolio needs to be comparable and equivalent to what a student has learned as a result of taking the course and earning a "C" grade or higher. Portfolios are rarely perfect; just as student term papers are rarely perfect. Here is the feedback Christine received from her portfolio assessor:

TABLE 1. *ASSESSOR'S EVALUATION*

Course Outcomes identified and Addressed	3 out of 4 points
Learning from Experience	4 out of 4 points
Understanding Theory and Practice	3 out of 4 points
Reflection	3 out of 4 point
Learning Application	4 out of 4 points
Communication	3 out of 4 points
Supporting Documentation	3 out of 4 points
TOTAL SCORE	**23 OUT OF 28 POINTS**

Assessor feedback:

I have reviewed your portfolio narrative and supporting documentation and find them to be appropriate and sufficient for the credit request. I appreciate the time you put in to developing your portfolio. Clearly you are a committed employee and have successfully developed appropriate communication skills.

Suggestions to improve your portfolio would be to provide a video clip of you delivering a briefing to reflect your oral communication skills. That was the major piece of supporting evidence that I found to be missing.

I wish you luck and success in your academic pursuits.

Credit Recommended: <u>3 Credits for Business Communication</u>

What Makes a Great Portfolio?

So far, we've reviewed two portfolios: one from Jacqueline for Purchasing Management and one from Christine for Business Communication. Here is what makes a great portfolio:

✓ A good introduction to set the context for the assessor
- Brief personal information
- Overview of learning and experiences that contributed to the development of the portfolio
- A general "laying out of the case" for credit

✓ Learning narrative in which the learning is aligned against specific learning objectives, outcomes, or competencies
  - Compelling college-level writing and composition
  - A learning narrative that has been checked, double-checked, and edited
  - Writing that has a "flow" organized by learning outcomes, with a chronology and references to documentation in a logical sequence
  - Excellent grammar, spelling, and sentence structure organized by thesis sentences
  - APA or other institutionally preferred academic style use throughout
  - The learning narrative is appropriate in length given the course; not overly wordy or too short to make the case
✓ An understanding of the difference between experience and experiential learning
  - Specific examples of learning from experience
  - Obvious reflection on the experience and the learning gained from it
  - Indication that the student can apply the learning to new situations or in different contexts
✓ Evidence of theoretical constructs or concepts that support the learning and practice
✓ Reference to how the learning might be developed and applied in the future
✓ The writing is supported with relevant and applicable references/citations
✓ Documentation makes the case for credit
  - Documentation is authentic and relevant
  - Documentation is linked to the writing in a coherent and logical fashion
  - Various forms of documentation are used to support the case for credit
✓ There is a conclusion or summary in the learning narrative that clearly illustrates to the assessor that the student is aware of the priorities for learning in the course and has emphasized them appropriately.
✓ The student does not plagiarize.

While some folks may be tempted to say, "I'll know a good portfolio when I see it," best practices call for using a rubric as a tool to ensure an accurate and fair assessment and to ensure that all of the above elements that make for a good portfolio are evidenced. Rubrics, when used by a faculty subject matter expert assessor, make the assessment process more transparent and less mysterious. In fact, it is recommended that students become familiar with the rubric before and during their portfolio development. This helps portfolio students stay on track. In fact, some students will self-select out of the portfolio development process when they see that they are not achieving optimum rubric scores based upon their own self-assessments. Please see Chapter 5 for more information on rubrics and other guidance on evaluating portfolios.

PORTFOLIO ASSESSMENT IN REAL LIFE

Developing a portfolio is not an intuitive process. Students must learn how to translate what they know and can do into academic language. Moreover, they almost need to think like assessors themselves in order to be successful. This chapter is all about the "inside story" of how students develop portfolios. It all starts with a conversation.

Step One: Advising Portfolio Students

Generally, for adult students there is an urgency to completing a postsecondary credential. Whether it is to complete their educations before their children, to avoid a job layoff situation, or simply to ensure a promotion or career change down the road. Adults are impatient. They are particularly impatient when they are faced with taking required courses with titles that sound like something they already know. For instance, Bill is the Executive Assistant to the Clerk of the Court, having earned the position after numerous years of legal support services with increasing responsibility. He is seeking a baccalaureate degree. When he sees "Introduction to Paralegal Studies," he is convinced he "knows the content of that course, and more." He mentions this to his admissions representative who then tells Bill about the possibility of developing a prior learning portfolio. Bill reviews the course and decides that if he is successful with the portfolio, he will be able to better leverage his time and money on courses that he really needs to take in subjects he does not already know.

It is important that a student know exactly how the portfolio credits might apply towards the degree. Some colleges have policies that limit the ways in which portfolio-earned credit can count in the degree plan (for example, as elective credit only). Students also need to make sure that they do not already have credit on the transcript that is on the topic in question. Therefore, Bill works with the admissions representative, as well as an academic advisor, to ensure that the credits he seeks will not be duplicative of the credits he has already earned and to make sure the college has policies that allow him to use portfolio-earned credit for major requirements. Once Bill has determined that his potential portfolio courses will count toward his degree requirements, he then registers for a portfolio course or workshop.

Bill also receives a student guide to portfolio assessment. This guide not only helps students understand portfolio assessment but is also highly useful to faculty and staff. It is a best practice to have a guide such as this. The guide includes information on how the process works as well as relevant academic policies, such as the appeals policy.

Step Two: The Portfolio Development Course or Workshop

There are several ways in which colleges and universities help students learn how to develop learning portfolios. The most common method is to provide a three-credit-hour course that empowers students to comprehend the difference between experience and learning as well as how to extract learning from their experiences through reflection and how to research courses to determine what learning is required in order to pass a course or courses. These portfolio courses also help students align their learning with an appropriate course (based upon the course syllabus). Students submit written assignments that prepare them to write the learning narrative in addition to giving them a clear understanding of how academic writing is different from the writing they may be doing at work. For some adults, a writing brush up is needed, and practice enables them to remember how to best organize their thoughts. Having the time to work with an instructor, as well as the support of a cohort of students with similar aspirations, supports students over the long, and sometimes arduous, hours of developing learning portfolios.

Some colleges offer non-credit workshops. Generally, one-half to one full day long, these workshops are a crash course in the mechanics of developing portfolios. There is not enough time to delve too deeply into learning theories or to practice writing. For experienced students (those with a few credit hours under their belts and/or who have taken English Composition already) the workshop is all they need to get started on their portfolios.

For an example of an online, self-directed, self-paced portfolio development course, please visit http://www.learningcounts.org/free-course-module/ where the first two modules of the course are available for free to give you an idea of what students learn as they go through portfolio development instruction. Additional information can be found at www.learningcounts.org.

Step Three: The Portfolio Development Process

Bill is a 35-year-old Executive Assistant to the Clerk of the Court. He has many years of experience providing administrative support to attorneys. He has already earned about 12 credit hours in general education. Here is a plan for Bill to develop his portfolio.

Developing a portfolio can take as long as a year or can be done as quickly as six weeks. Much is dependent upon how many credits a student is seeking, the ease of finding documentation, and how experienced the student is at writing and making the case for credit. Here is a general work plan for completing a portfolio for one course. We'll use Bill's **Introduction to Paralegal Studies** course.

BILL'S PORTFOLIO DEVELOPMENT PLAN

Time Frame	Activity	Deliverables
Week One	Read about different kinds of learning, including informal and formal learning. Develop a timeline to capture learning that can help in identifying possible areas for which credit might be sought.	Prepare a timeline of formal and informal learning or a learning inventory. Request previous transcripts. Request previous professional development records and determine who might write a letter of verification for him.

(Continued)

Time Frame	Activity	Deliverables
Week Two	Identify the course for which credit is sought. We've already determined that Bill is seeking credit for **Introduction to Paralegal Studies.** Find the course syllabus. Consider other courses within this discipline that may be applicable. Find course descriptions.	Outline for portfolio structure including notes on where to find documentation and who to contact for it.
Week Three	If possible, double-check with an academic advisor that the course(s) selected for the portfolio will apply toward degree requirements and are approved to earn credit by portfolio. Learn about Bloom's Taxonomy and Kolb's Cycle of Learning.	Contact third parties for documentation related to the course(s).
Week Four	Write an outline for the learning narrative in alignment with the course objectives, outcomes, or competencies from the syllabus. Consider specific examples of experiential learning.	Learning narrative outline Include logical locations for documentation links.
Week Five	Add theory to the learning narrative outline. Check out textbooks from the library as referenced on the syllabus.	Review the various topics covered in the text as well as referenced on the syllabus to ensure familiarity with all aspects of the learning outcomes or objectives. Reflect on how textbook concepts link to real life work situations. Analyze and synthesize the information with his own experiential learning.
Week Six	Complete first draft of the learning narrative. Organize the portfolio, including where the student will reference documentation throughout the narrative.	Organize documentation from various sources. First draft of learning narrative, including documentation links
Following Weeks	Seek input from a writing lab or colleague on the first draft. Edit and revise first draft to final draft. Double- and triple-check the learning narrative to ensure all learning outcomes have been addressed. Ensure all experiences have been tied to learning outcomes and that writing does not veer off into experiences only. Check to see that reflection is evident. Add citations and documentation. Submit portfolio for assessment.	Complete portfolio and submit for assessment.

Students should have some college experience before developing a portfolio. Preparing a portfolio is easier when students are familiar with how courses are organized and how to use the syllabus. They also should have taken an English Composition course or have solid writing experience due to the intensive writing required. Student outcomes are better if the student has taken a college writing course before embarking on portfolio development. This information should be made available within all communications describing the portfolio assessment processes.

Step Four: The Assessment

Once a portfolio is submitted, a student should no longer be able to make edits or provide additional information to the portfolio. Institutional policies and procedures should clearly articulate any rules regarding portfolio submission. Some institutions help ensure faculty assessors receive the portfolios for evaluation only after they have received a top-level review of it to determine if it is worthy of being assigned a faculty assessor or not. Reviews are typically conducted by a portfolio assessment coordinator or director. This review is based upon the organization of the portfolio; the clarity with which it addresses learning outcomes, objectives, or competencies; and for general grammar and spelling checks. Portfolios that are not well written or that do not follow portfolio guidelines should be returned to the student for further development. Portfolios that meet the guidelines are ready for the assessment.

The next step is to assign the portfolio to a faculty subject matter expert (preferably one who has received training or professional development in how to evaluate a portfolio). The faculty subject matter expert, or assessor, should have extensive experience in the discipline, including having likely taught the course before. With this knowledge and experience, the assessor clearly knows the expectations for students who pass the course when taken online or in a traditional classroom format.

The assessor evaluates the portfolio to determine if the student has achieved equivalent and comparable learning. Best practice dictates the use of an established faculty-developed rubric so that all portfolios are assessed on the same merits. If the portfolio is deemed credit worthy, the assessor will provide the approval and return the portfolio back to an administrator. The assessor will have provided critical feedback on the portfolio so that the student can continue to learn from the portfolio assessment process. Students who miss the "C" or better assessment may wish to continue working on the portfolio and resubmit it later for a second assessment if allowed by institutional policy. Other students who have essentially failed the course via portfolio are encouraged to take the course, rather than attempt to do another portfolio.

Data should be collected to determine the institution's credit/no credit portfolio assessment rates. If the fail rate is higher than 30 percent, then your portfolio assessment advising and course or workshop should be reviewed. Because portfolio assessment is so demanding, students generally self-select out of the process if they believe they do not have the college-level learning required or if the writing is intimidating. This trend leads to higher pass rates—between 70 and 80 percent.

Student portfolios that do not earn credit are not transcripted onto the student record. Only successful portfolios make it onto the transcript. However, if the student fails the portfolio development course, then that "F" will appear on the transcript.

Portfolio Appeals

Occasionally, a student will believe that her/his portfolio was unfairly denied credit. An appeals process is necessary to provide the student with due process. Generally speaking, adherence to a rubric makes the appeal unnecessary. However, some students will persist. In the case of an appeal, the portfolio is generally routed to a different faculty subject matter expert for a new assessment. If there is a variance, then a third assessor is brought in to review the portfolio. Second assessors should be unaware of the status of the portfolio, only knowing that it needs to be assessed. If the additional assessments come back with credit denied, then the student is once again denied credit. Of course, feedback from the assessment will help the student to understand why credit was not granted.

Step Five: Student Feedback

A strong portfolio assessment program collects data on how students perceive the experience. Ensure your program has planned data collection protocols. This might include student evaluations of their portfolio development course or workshop and a survey or evaluation of the portfolio assessment process itself. Student feedback will help you assure your messaging regarding portfolio assessment is clear and compelling.

Program Oversight

Portfolio assessment data collection is an important aspect of administering a high quality portfolio assessment program. Here are some data points that are useful in providing adequate oversight:

Data	Trend Information
Number of credits awarded per student	How many credits are awarded per student? What is the most credit that has been awarded and how frequently? What is the credit awarded/credit denied rate?
Most often requested courses	Are courses being requested for certain academic programs or majors? How are the credits used—for electives, general education, or to meet major/degree requirements?
Portfolio student academic outcomes	When portfolio students earn credits for prerequisites, how do they perform in subsequent courses? Do they have higher persistence and graduation rates, as the national research indicates? How do their GPAs compare to non-portfolio students?
Assessor statistics	How many portfolios are assigned to assessors? Which assessors are assessing the most portfolios? Are there trends?
Timing	What is the assessor turnaround time for portfolios? Are there peak times for portfolios? Are portfolios completed by first-year students?

Another important aspect of oversight is diligently monitoring portfolios for plagiarism. The ease of cutting and pasting from the Internet cannot be overlooked. It can, and does, happen. Decide if portfolios fit into your institutional academic honesty policy or if a new portfolio policy needs to be created. Consider using a plagiarism detection service such as *turnitin.com*. It is also recommended that you ask the student to sign an Academic Honesty Statement to accompany portfolios upon submission for assessment.

Integrity is key to a high quality portfolio assessment program. Integrity can also be assured by adhering to the **CAEL Quality Principles** (see Appendix B). It can be enhanced with process transparency, such as (1) sharing the assessment rubric (see next chapter) with students, (2) providing a workshop or course to teach students how to articulate and align their learning using a course match method for portfolio development, (3) ensuring all students receive a Portfolio Assessment Policy Guide, and (4) posting success rates and frequently asked questions for portfolio (and others) students to manage expectations for the assessment process. Integrity can also be strengthened by providing ongoing professional development for faculty, academic advisors, admissions representatives, registrar, financial aid/veterans affairs, and business office staff. Emphasize at every point that credit is only awarded for college-level learning—not for experience.

CAEL (Council for Adult and Experiential Learning) provides professional development workshops, training sessions, and webinars for faculty, staff, and PLA program coordinators or directors.

Student Portfolio Example #3—Bill

PARA 2010-81—Introduction to Paralegal Studies—3 Credit Hours[7]

I. Introduction

a. Background

I am a 35-year-old non-lawyer legal professional with over a decade of experience in providing quality support to attorneys and clients. My career began as a receptionist and

---

[7] This portfolio is used with permission from the author.

calendaring clerk at a personal injury firm, but they quickly tapped me to be a support professional. There, and with the firms that followed, I gained a significant amount of experience and knowledge in the field. I progressed from answering the phones to managing complex, multi-million dollar cases from inception to appeal. One year ago, I took my education in this industry to the civil servant side and joined the federal US District Court in ABC as the Executive Assistant to the Clerk of the Court. The Clerk acts as the Chief Executive Officer for the court and oversees all non-judicial issues with the court. Here, my learning has happily continued, and I am thrilled to augment my knowledge base.

Interestingly, this love of the legal profession began at a young age—when I was 11 years old, I shadowed a judge located in a small town in Colorado where I lived at the time. The Honorable Judge was gracious in allowing a curious youngster to observe proceedings in court and chambers, and I will always be grateful to him for the exposure and education.

I have a sharp, analytical mind, which is suited for the legal profession. In addition to my job at the US District Court for the Northern District of ABC, I am presently working toward obtaining my undergraduate degree and just completed my first full year.

b. Supporting Documentation

In support of this learning assessment portfolio, I will refer to the following documents:

Document 1: LinkedIn Profile (including skill endorsements)

[Includes all of his positions from Assistant to the Clerk to Litigation Secretary, as well as endorsements and four written recommendations]

Document 2: Letter of Verification from John Doe, Esq.

[Includes an extensive description of Bill's work including general paralegal skills, legal research, legal writing, legal ethics, technology support, law firm management, and litigation sections written on a law firm's letterhead and signed by an attorney]

Document 3: USCourts.gov Chart re Federal and State Court Systems

Document 4: Docket Sheet from Name, Inc. v. Someone, et al, District of ABC, Case No. XXX

Document 5: Plaintiff Name, Inc.'s Memorandum of Law in Support of Its Motion for Summary Judgment, filed XXXXX in Name, Inc. v. Someone, et al. District of ABC, Case No. XXX.

c. Presentation of the Course I Am Petitioning for Credit

i. **Course Title:** Introduction to Paralegal Studies

ii. **Course Prefix & Number:** PARA 2010-81

iii. **Course Credits:** 3

iv. **Course Description:** *Introduction to the study of law and the legal system; an overview of the skills of the paralegal including litigation, legal interviewing, investigation in the law office, and legal trends, emphasizing professionalism and ethics, including the unauthorized practice of law.*

v. **Course Objectives**

1. *Describe the paralegal profession in the context of the US legal system and current ethical, regulatory, educational, and workplace issues*

2. *Identify distinguishing characteristics of the federal and state court systems*

3. *Correctly utilize basic legal terminology and vocabulary*

4. *Develop beginning legal analysis skills*

5. *Demonstrate a basic understanding of legal research and writing*

6. *Provide an overview of criminal and civil litigation*

7. *Explain informal and formal advocacy techniques, including mediation*

8. *Summarize paralegal investigative techniques utilizing legal rules of evidence*

d. Statement of Purpose and Format

In this learning narrative, I will demonstrate that I have absorbed the contents of the learning objectives of the course through work experience and reflection. I will address each learning objective individually, except I will combine topics 3–5 as they are heavily intertwined.

As discussed above, based on my high-performing career in the industry, I believe that I hold the knowledge, both theoretical and applied, on these topics.

II. Course Learning

a. Objective No. 1: Describe the paralegal profession in the context of the US legal system and current ethical, regulatory, educational, and workplace issues.

Paralegals are a critical and expected piece of the United States legal environment. A hybrid of skills above an administrative assistant but below an attorney, paralegals bill out their time to clients but at much lower rates than lawyers. One respected source describes paralegal work as "performing substantive legal tasks (i.e., non-clerical)," to such a degree that courts often award fees for both attorneys' and paralegals' time to prevailing parties, when appropriate (Larbalestrier 2009, p. 15).

I observed through my work at law firms that clients often use paralegals as a cost containment measure. This is usually great for everyone involved as the client saves money, the attorneys' schedules are freed up for more complex issues, and the firm still makes a profit. However, there are still pitfalls. Paralegals are prohibited from the practice of law and must therefore remain vigilant to potential requests that exceed their authority.

In addition, I learned that there are a plethora of different paraprofessionals in the field and vary by specialization, similar to their attorney counterparts. For instance, a family law paralegal is very different from an in-house counsel's paralegal. While their foundational skills are likely similar, their careers will be shaped by their practice.

This knowledge was most often put into practice when strategizing regarding staffing for specific cases or projects. I assisted in case and hearings across the country and helped my attorneys select the appropriate paralegals for the matter at hand (see Document 2, Letter of Verification, p. 1).

b. Objective No. 2: Identify distinguishing characteristics of federal and state court systems.

Basic jurisdictional issues are important to understand and not something that a layperson is typically familiar with. There are many different characteristics between federal and state jurisdictions, but what it boils down is who has the "right" to hear and adjudicate a conflict. My employer, the United States Courts, has an excellent and concise chart (see Document 3, Comparaison Chart, p. 1) explaining the differences between these courts, and imparts that "...due to federalism, both the federal government and each of the state governments have their own courts systems" (United States Courts, n.d., para. 2).

At the beginning of my career, the majority of the cases I worked on were under the umbrella of state court laws: personal injury matters (mostly car and motorcycle accidents), employment discrimination, and medical malpractice suits. Later in my career, and presently, I became much more comfortable with federal cases, which involve national statutes, laws, and controversies (see Document 1, LinkedIn Profile).

After absorbing a lot of legal wisdom from attorneys that I worked with, I am now able to analyze a case and make recommendations to attorneys on which court to file an action in. Additionally, I now work squarely in the federal jurisdiction at a trial court, and questions of jurisdiction are often brought to my court for review. One of the most sensational cases to come out of this court in recent history is the same sex marriage case, or "the Prop 8 case." The Supreme Court ultimately decided that it didn't have jurisdiction to hear the arguments of the parties, thereby allowing the lower court's ruling to stand (*Hollingsworth v. Perry* 2013).

c. Objective No. 3: Correctly utilize basic legal terminology and vocabulary.

Objective No. 4: Develop beginning legal analysis skills.

Objective No. 5: Demonstrate a basic understanding of legal research writing.

I have combined these three topics because they necessarily overlap and flow together. My first law firm, the Attorney Law Firm[8], was an educational "boot camp" on these topics and I am grateful for the hands-on learning. At my first firm, I was exposed to the proper use of legal and court terms, initiated my legal analysis abilities, and they allowed me to practice research and writing (see Document 1, LinkedIn Profile).

One of the great aspects of providing support in a law firm is that you get to learn from and observe incredibly gifted writers. Even prior to drafting on my own, I acquired so much knowledge simply by inputting attorney edits into documents. After a while and with some mentoring from the attorneys, it became clear to me that legal writing boils down to two basic tenets: be concise and be persuasive.

Once these skills became refined, attorneys often called upon me to make initial drafts of legal documents for the court, clients, and vendors (see Document 2, Letter of Verification, p. 1). While I am capable of drafting routine documents with ease, I also enjoy challenges—one time an attorney asked me to draft an entire motion to compel production of documents. I am pleased to say that he made very few edits before sending it to the partnership for review. I am blessed in that I continue to work with great wordsmiths, and that I remain educated by observing and absorbing their work.

Bill attached actual work samples as his documentation. Using work samples can be compelling for the assessors when linked directly to the required course outcomes or objectives. He also includes a Letter of Verification that speaks directly to his learning and skills.

To further demonstrate my knowledge in this area, I have attached the docket of a complex case that I worked from inception to appeal regarding an airline's right to serve alcoholic beverages in federal airspace over the objection of the state below the airspace in question (see Document 4, Docket). I was chiefly responsible for the final drafting and filing of each of the briefs filed by the Plaintiff (the airline) in this matter, which included an analysis of the cases cited by the attorneys and insuring their correct citation in the briefs. One of the largest legal filings that I worked on requested judgement in favor of the airline, or a Motion for Summary Judgment (see Document 5, Motion). The second table at the beginning of the document, the Table of Authorities, is a concise list of all authorities listed in the brief (whether in support or against the client's position). I created this table after solidifying and correcting all of the cases and statutes cited by the attorneys.

---

[8] The Law Firm is not identified to protect the student's privacy.

d. Objective No. 6: Provide an overview of criminal and civil litigation.

The differences between criminal and civil litigation are vast enough to nearly be different fields of study. There are entirely different sets of rules and procedures governing these two case types, and even a separate lexicon in many respects. *Findlaw,* a respected online legal resource, succinctly states that "crimes are generally offenses against the state, and are accordingly prosecuted by the state. Civil cases on the other hand, are typically disputes between individuals regarding the legal duties and responsibilities they owe one another" (FindLaw, n.d., para. 1).

Although civil cases are mired in the milieu of our country's issues—petitioning the courts for assistance to resolve disputes—I prefer to work on them more than criminal cases. Typically (and perhaps dishearteningly?), civil cases are larger and more complex than their criminal cousins, although there are notable exceptions to that generalization. The bulk of my experience has been working in civil cases, including but not limited to, personal injury, employment discrimination, medical malpractice, mass torts, product liability and securities class actions, constitutional and preemption law. I believe I could jump into any civil case and hit the ground running (see Document 2, Letter of Verification). However, I have a little experience in criminal cases when I assisted a former colleague with her caseload. She is a solo criminal defense attorney and had a period of being overwhelmed with work. The attorney actually flew me down for a few weekends to help her get on top of her trial and appellate preparations. I was happy to help a friend, learn a new type of law, and travel all at the same time.

At my present position, I work with a large inmate population on both of these case types. Obviously prior to becoming inmates, criminal charges are filed against them and those cases take a natural course. If convicted, the inmate may have a grievance with the prison or prison staff and then they file a civil complaint in court.

e. Objective No. 7: Explain informal and formal advocacy techniques, including mediation.

Of course, for any case to be resolved, criminal or civil, it takes much more than the courts by themselves—it takes advocacy on all sides as well. It is clear to me that it is beneficial for all parties to explore multiple paths to resolution. The ability to utilize non-judicial forms of case resolution, such as mediation or arbitration, saves time, money, and resources for everyone, including the government.

Over the course of my career, I learned that in order to obtain the best possible results for a client, it is necessary to "build up" a case when drafting a mediation or arbitration statement. For instance, a client may have lost wages in the range of $10,000 to $25,000 depending on several factors. Because the other side will attack every statement and contentious point, it is important to start at the high end of $25,000 in order to protect your client and his or her losses as much as possible. Then, when engaging in alternative dispute resolution (also known as "ADR"), both sides will have room to negotiate somewhere in the middle of the range.

On a personal note, I enjoy the settlement process because I view myself as non-legal mediator, and I enjoy the looks of relief on most parties' faces when they walk away with a case on the way out of the door.

f. Objective No. 8: Summarize paralegal investigative techniques utilizing legal rules of evidence.

The Rules of Evidence are a large tome of imperative rules regarding what can be shown to courts and juries (often described as "admissible" or "inadmissible" evidence). The

Federal Rules of Evidence, which are similar to individual states' rules, are complex and intimidating (Cornell Law School, n.d.).

Fully understanding the Rules of Evidence is nearly a career unto itself, and upon reflection, I believe that my own knowledge and application of them slowly continues to expand. As an example, one of the most commonly heard rules of evidences is often splashed about on television: hearsay. Hearsay is defined as "something heard from another person" or "something that you have been told" (Hearsay, n.d., [Def.1]). This may sound simple, but when you have to put this knowledge into practice and analyze every word that a witness is or may be saying, that simple definition quickly becomes a complex beast.

At my first law firm, I reviewed evidence, including police reports, and made preliminary recommendations regarding admissibility to attorneys based upon my basic understanding of the rules of evidence. For example, once I reviewed statements from a witness at a motorcycle accident who said she saw the accident happen but the police report stated that the same witness heard the crash and the noise caused her to turn her head. In that instance, it was not admissible to say that she saw the accident. In this scenario, the witness heard the accident and she saw its aftermath.

III. **Conclusion**

I believe that I have shown in this narrative that I understand the basic concepts of being a paralegal in the United States. Specifically, I have demonstrated an understanding of where paraprofessionals fit into the legal industry, and that I have a firm grasp on their basic duties and obligations. I will continue to hone this knowledge for the rest of my career as I feel strongly that I will be involved in the courts or another aspect of the legal field until my retirement.

Here are Bill's references for his citations:

References

Cornell Law School. n.d. *Federal rules of evidence.* Retrieved from http://www.law.cornell.edu/rules/fre

FindLaw. n.d. *The differences between a criminal case and a civil case.* Retrieved from http://criminal.findlaw.com/criminal-law-basics/the-differences-between-a-criminal-case-and-a-civil-case.html

Hearsay [Def. 1]. n.d. *Merriam-Webster online.* In Merriam-Webster. Retrieved from http://www.Merriam-webster.com/dictionary/hearsay

Hollingsworth v. Perry, 570 U.S. __ 2013

Larbalestrier, D. 2009. *Paralegal practice & procedure.* New York, NY: Prentice Hall Press

United States Courts. n.d. *Comparing state and federal courts.* Retrieved from http://www.uscourts.gov/educational-resources/get-informed/federal-court-basics/comparing-state-federal-courts.aspx

Bill's portfolio also included all of the documentation that he referred to throughout his portfolio. While Bill's portfolio is heavy on application and perhaps light on the theoretical constructs, paralegal studies is a technical course. Clearly, Bill's knowledge and experience aligns well with the course. His documentation is very strong, particularly the letter of verification from an attorney for which Bill worked for three years. Bill earned three credit hours for this portfolio.

Example of an Excellent Letter of Verification

Company Letterhead

Dear Portfolio Evaluator:

My name is John Doe, and I am General Counsel USA for *ABC*, one of the world's premier Scotch and spirits producers. Prior to joining *ABC*, I was a partner at two top international AmLaw firms, where I specialized in complex constitutional, regulatory, compliance, and preemption issues at all levels nationwide and in some international markets. I have been a leading advisor for the wine industry on a variety of issues but have also interacted with other heavily-regulated sectors including airlines, healthcare, pharmaceuticals, and oil.

At one of these firms, Bill was my extraordinary assistant for three years. In addition to handling the tasks typical of a legal administrative professional with care and attention, Bill is also very intelligent, engaged, and a creative problem solver. He was directly involved in my cases, and he displayed tact and judgment dealing with high level clients, attorneys, judges, and management. Bill has the ability to grasp and analyze complex data, a rock solid work ethic, and he was often a mentor and a leader to his peers.

Bill's breadth of tacit knowledge in the legal field is significant, and I am pleased to describe his skills in depth here:

General Paralegal Skills

While Bill did not hold the official title of paralegal because of stringent certification requirements, he often met or exceeded the skills of senior paralegals at the firm and was often involved in coaching them on systems. Bill demonstrates a clear understanding of state and federal court systems, legal terminology, and he is adept at applying legal analysis to relevant fact patterns. As outlined below, Bill is also capable of advanced legal research and writing, and he is very familiar with all levels of advocacy, including pre-investigative research, alternative dispute resolution, and hearings at trial and appellate levels. Bill was requested by both attorneys and clients to assist at hearings across the country.

Legal Research

Legal research is a specific niche and talent which often requires the ability to think "outside the box" in order to find a similar case or statute which supports your client's position. I often called on Bill to find cases, statutes, regulations, and articles via Westlaw, LexisNexis, or jurisdictional databases. He also learned how to provide succinct case summaries and even his own opinion on how they might impact the present matter. Bill was also in charge of finalizing volumes of legal briefs before they were submitted to the court, and a key aspect of that position is to correct legal citations and to build a table of authorities.

Legal Writing

Bill is very skilled at following the two key principles of legal writing: be concise and be persuasive. Bill assisted me in developing case and brief outlines, and was helpful in sticking to the standard formula for legal writing: describe the facts, state the applicable legal standard, apply the standard to the facts, and then summarize the issue. Bill very capably accessed the "Blue Book," which is the bible for standard legal citations. He often assisted in the drafting and revision of legal documents, from case inception to appeals and everything in between. Bill absorbed information on this topic very well and made substantive, relevant editing suggestions for correspondence and legal documents. Bill also served as a final proofreader and editor for formatting, grammar, spelling, and citations.

Legal Ethics

Legal ethics is a broad topic and can serve as a career by itself. I have a solid background in this subject from serving as a primary legal and policy advisor to the Office of the Chief Trial Counsel for the State Bar, with particular emphasis on high-profile attorney ethics cases. In the context of a paralegal or litigation assistant, a foundational understanding of the potential ethical issues is necessary in two ways: 1) a client may ask a firm to do something on its behalf which raises eyebrows, and 2) conflicts of interest may arise and need to be immediately identified. While attorney-client privilege bars me from providing specific information here, I can attest that Bill had a quick grasp of any issues that arose and discussed them with me appropriately. Bill worked through many conflict checks via a giant database of potential issues, and he became very familiar with the proper application of Rules of Professional Conduct for both attorneys and paralegal professionals.

Technology Support

Bill has mastered a wide variety of software programs utilized in the legal industry, and he often trained other staff or attorneys on them. These programs are highly specialized and require the ability to interact with them while keeping the client, expenses, and the case in mind. For Bill, this list includes, but is not limited to, discovery management applications such as Concordance or Summation, networked document management systems, trial and litigation support software, programs designed to assist in law firm management and billing, and electronic pleading submissions to courts and mediators. Bill is also an advanced user of Microsoft Suite, especially Word, Excel, and PowerPoint. As a result of his work in litigation, he was very sensitive to issues relating to privileged client and attorney-client information, and ensured that relevant information was treated appropriately.

Law Firm Management

Any business model has its own challenges when it comes to management and administration, and law firms are not exception. Bill demonstrated great acumen at learning the ins and outs of our firm's policies and procedures, following them strictly, while balancing operational needs. Bill has a wealth of experience understanding firm and client trust accounts, timekeeping, pre-bill and bill review, business development endeavors, records management and retention systems, and utilizing proprietary intranet systems typical to law firms and large corporate clients.

Litigation

This is the realm where Bill shines brightest. Bill is able to jump into any part of a case time-line and excel at whatever needs to be done. I have worked with him through each of these phases, including pre-filing investigation, initial responsive filings (Complaints, Answers, or other responsive pleadings), discovery (including protective orders), law and motion (including substantive and complex summary judgment motions), trial court hearings, and appellate briefing and hearings. Bill takes exceptional care in determining proper calendaring for deadlines and procedurals issues throughout the litigation process.

While we worked on a number of cases and development matters together, the key cases that I managed with Bill's assistance are listed below:

[three actual cases listed here including one described in Bill's Narrative]

Each of these matters involved complex facts, Constitutional or federal preemption laws, and high-profile clients. Bill was the main point person for any case files, organization and coordination—he truly "owned" them and took pride in his remarkable ability to support me and other attorneys through the life of these matters.

In closing, I cannot recommend Bill highly enough for your positive review of his portfolio in any of these areas. Bill is fully capable of not only engaging in each of the topics I have described, but he would be an excellent instructor for them as well, and I believe that shows the depth of his education in this arena.

Thank you for your time. If you have any questions, please call me.

Very truly yours,

John Doe Signature Here

John Doe, Esq.

Bill's portfolio was assessed as credit worthy. Bill earned three credits for his portfolio.

For Bill's Portfolio (Introduction to Paralegal Studies)

Rubric Score: 26 out of 28

RUBRIC SCORES

Course Outcomes Identified and Addressed	4/4
Learning from Experience	3/4
Understanding of Theory and Practice	4/4
Reflection	3/4
Learning Application	4/4
Communication	3/4
Supporting Documentation	4/4

ASSESSOR WRITTEN FEEDBACK

Bill's legal experience is substantial, although he lacks information about criminal law. His learning narrative is stronger in some areas than in others in substantiating his experience in and understanding of each of the learning objectives for the Introduction to Paralegal Studies course. He clearly understands the difference between federal and state courts and is able to accurately use legal terms and phrases. He freely admits that his knowledge of criminal law is weak, but it is an area that he will likely strengthen with further career experience.

He does not elaborate about the variety of informal advocacy techniques. He understands mediation but does not mention arbitration, which is often used in both state and federal courts. It is unclear if he has any experience with any of the informal advocacy techniques.

Overall, his experience is expansive and the support he has received through the letter of verification from Attorney John Doe is impressive. He would be overqualified as a student in a beginning paralegal course—and likely could teach most of the course.

Effective Feedback

Students spend a great deal of time and effort preparing portfolios. The process is high stakes for them given the potential to earn college credits. Understanding that many students have spent weeks, even months, writing about and documenting their learning, it is reasonable for them to expect some written feedback on their portfolios beyond the credit/no credit decision. Written feedback should be thoughtful, encouraging, and specific. Students should be told what they have done well and where the narrative or documentation could be improved. Recommendations for continued learning are always important. Assessor feedback is most helpful to students when assessors keep in mind that the assessment is about learning (see Appendix B).

Examples of Good Assessor Feedback

For Jacqueline's Portfolio (Purchasing Management)

Rubric Score: 28 out of 28

ASSESSOR WRITTEN FEEDBACK

The student lists each of the course outcomes for BA-390 Purchasing Management and presents evidence of understanding for each of the deliverables. She has had a career rich in experience and has come up through the ranks on the purchasing side from a time when purchasing was considered an "add-on" function of the storeroom clerk to its current professional status. She has demonstrated her competence by earning the designation of Certified Purchasing Manager (CPM). She has shown evidence of benchmarking against other comparable establishments, cost savings, critical thinking, ethics, using GANTT charts, value engineering, and the value of thinking strategically in the narrative.

The student was able to show evidence of learning skills; gaining experience in one position and using that skill in a future, more responsible purchasing function. A letter from the vice president of her company also served as strong evidence of how she leveraged her knowledge base.

For Christine's Portfolio (Business Communications)

Rubric Score: 23 out of 28

ASSESSOR WRITTEN FEEDBACK

I have reviewed your portfolio narrative and supporting documentation and find them to be appropriate and sufficient for the credit request. I appreciate the time you put into developing your portfolio. Clearly, you are a committed employee and have successfully developed appropriate communication skills.

Suggestions to improve your portfolio would be to provide a video clip of you delivering a briefing to reflect your oral communication skills. That was the major piece of supporting evidence I found missing.

I wish you luck and success in your academic pursuits.

Another Student's Portfolio (Project Management)

Rubric Score: 22 out of 28

ASSESSOR WRITTEN FEEDBACK

I have reviewed your learning narrative and was impressed with the successes you have made in your work experience. The objective of the narrative is to document the equivalent of college-level learning.

Thank you for sharing your varied background and extensive work experience. You provided documentation to support your portfolio including your narrative, transcript, and PMI certification. The documentation somewhat articulates the learning derived from the courses you took, the things you know, and what you have learned on the job. I see that you have PMI certification, for example; but I don't know anything about the scope and nature of the projects you have managed. You might have added more documentation that specifically talks to the programs and projects you have managed, such as work examples and a description of the successes and challenges that you have faced related to Project Management.

For the most part, your narrative was thorough, well organized, and followed a logical sequence. I liked the way you organized your narrative clearly around the course objectives.

Your narrative describes concepts you learned and what you know, but doesn't provide relevant examples to fully demonstrate this learning and how you learned by experience. You did not cite any specifics about your experience or provide concrete examples. You demonstrated a clear ability to apply theory but didn't really tie this well to your experience. You did not demonstrate an ability to apply your learning to other contexts. You did not really discuss how this knowledge has been transferred to other environments. You may have these abilities, but it is not described in the narrative.

Finally, your communication in the narrative is at an acceptable level, including strong thesis statements and arguments that follow a logical order, but there were numerous syntactical and word choice errors and omissions.

The documentation provided supports awarding credit for QSO 340 Project Management. You possess the skills necessary for mastery of the requirements of this course.

Note: This student was awarded credit. The portfolio is clearly not perfect, but deemed to be worthy of credit.

5

ASSURING QUALITY ASSESSMENT

Assuring a quality assessment process requires ongoing oversight and professional development for faculty. Best practices dictate that assessors be assigned portfolios based upon their subject matter expertise, traditional faculty credentials, experience teaching the course or courses for which credit is being sought, as well as a willingness to complete the assessment within an agreed upon timeframe. Generally reviewed in assessor professional development workshops, it is important for assessors to be familiar with experiential learning theories and adult learning perspectives.

Assessing adult learners is based upon five basic constructs, or tenets (Kasworm and Marienau, 1997; Fiddler, Marienau, and Whitaker 2006).

Five Tenets of Adult-Oriented Assessment and Related Propositions about Learning[9]

Five Tenets		What It Means for Portfolio Assessment
1. Learning is derived from multiple sources.	Adults are not likely to have had the same learning experiences as young people in college courses. Their lives are complex, and they pick up learning from many venues.	*Adult experiences that lead to learning, as evidenced in portfolios, is experiential and sometimes a result of training. The learning may include having read textbooks and trade journals.*
2. Learning engages the whole person and contributes to that person's development.	Learning is a critical mediator of development; maturation is the expansion of the qualities that define individual differences.	*Portfolios show the learning progression from initial experience to the acquisition of learning. Every portfolio is unique.*
3. Learning and the capacity for self-direction are promoted by feedback.	Adulthood brings an expanding capacity for self-motivation, self-directed learning, and self-assessment. Adults need feedback from their practice in order to move forward with learning. However, just because a student is an adult does not mean they have learned by virtue of age alone.	*By virtue of choosing to develop a portfolio, adults demonstrate self-motivation. The experience of writing lends itself to self-directed learning, self-assessment, and self-reflection.*

(Continued)

---

[9] The title of this table and the first two columns are the work of C. Kasworm and C. Marienau picked up from their adapted version on page 10 of the second edition of *Assessing Learning: Standards, Principles, & Procedures* by M. Fiddler, C. Marienau, and U. Whitaker. The third column was added by the author.

Five Tenets		What It Means for Portfolio Assessment
4. Learning occurs in context; its significance relates in part to its influence on those contexts.	The contexts of which we are a part and that we create as adults become increasingly indistinguishable; among the defining features of adulthood are the kind and extent of responsibilities that adults assume and that set many of the contexts for meaningful learning.	*Assessors look for a student's ability to transfer learning to different contexts, leveraging what is known to develop new learning and more sophisticated reflection leading to deeper understanding.*
5. Learning from experience is a unique meaning-making event that creates diversity among adults.	Adults grow more unique and diverse in relation to each other; the richer the experience, the greater the potential for meaningful learning.	*Rarely does a portfolio fail to show insight into the personal journey of making meaning out of life's challenges and obstacles. This diversity of experience makes for fascinating reading.*

FIGURE 3. *Five Tenets*

Many adults learn as practitioners first. Therefore, their experiential education starts out highly focused and applied. Portfolios provide a view into adult learning styles. As their education progresses, they add breadth to their learning and enjoy discovering the theory or conceptual framework behind what they have experienced. College curricula, as organized from first-year lower level courses through the senior year of more in-depth upper division courses, tend to focus first on the theories and constructs of the discipline before discussing the application or "real life" or experiential aspects of the discipline.

For students who are fortunate enough to go to college straight from high school, their learning is dictated by the curricula. It is only when they have an opportunity for an internship or work in their fields of study that they are able to apply their learning in context.

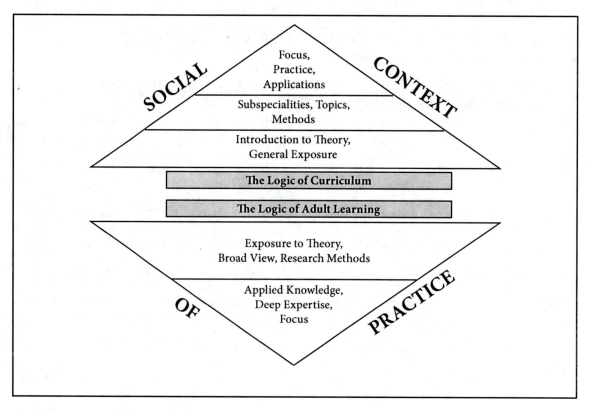

FIGURE 4. *Evidence of Learning*

Working With the Rubric

Sample Assessment Rubric

Here you can see what a portfolio assessment rubric might look like.

Criteria	4 Exceptional Performance	3 Above Average Performance	2 Addressed, but Room for Improvement	0 Not addressed or Not acceptable
Course Objectives, Learning Outcomes, or Competencies Identified and Addressed				
Learning from Experience				
Understanding Theory and Practice				
Reflection Is Evident				
Learning Application				
College-Level Writing and Communication				
Supporting Documentation				

Total Score _____ (maximum score is 28)

Credit Recommendation

☐ Credit Recommended
☐ Credit Denied

Written Feedback for Student

_____
_____
_____
_____
_____

To see actual completed assessment, go to Appendix C.

FIGURE 5. *Sample Rubric*

The rubric can be as sophisticated or as simple as is preferable by the faculty and must be understandable by students and assessors. The rubric must emphasize the desired outcomes for the various criteria being assessed. Some rubrics may weigh certain criteria more than other criteria. In portfolio assessment, the student can only earn credit for the course if he or she earns the equivalent of a "C" or better on the rubric, generally defined as 70 percent or greater. All behaviors and expectations should be clearly articulated for the assessor to be able to easily see where the student's portfolio falls on the grading scale. The criteria, on the other hand, represent the key learning outcomes and expectations of students taking the course. Examples beyond what the sample rubric displays might be college-level writing, evidence of critical thinking, clearly differentiating between learning and experience, and more.

LearningCounts, CAEL's national online nonprofit portfolio assessment service, uses one standard rubric that is applicable for all portfolios. The subject matter experts (faculty assessors) use the rubric's general measures of competencies, outcomes, or objectives on which to apply to the relevant content of their disciplines to bring the rubric to life. The use of a common rubric works very well for students and assessors. Rubrics can be developed course by course, but this adds to the complexity of the work as well as possibly using more faculty resources over time.

Checks and Balances

All high quality portfolio assessment programs have a series of routine checks and balances. These activities may include any or all of the following:

✓ **Adherence to the CAEL Quality Principles for Assessment** (see Appendix A)

Quality portfolio assessment programs use the 10 Quality Principles for Assessment as a foundation for both academic and administrative policies for prior learning assessment. Accrediting bodies often look to these principles when working with institutions on prior learning assessment.

✓ **Staff review of portfolios prior to being submitted to an assessor**

Designing a process that enables a cursory review of portfolios prior to being given to an assessor is a smart way to catch portfolios that are not of high quality. Students who have received some education on how to develop portfolios generally submit portfolios that are ready for the assessor. However, occasionally a student just does not have the skills to submit a portfolio and should not be asked to pay for an assessment if the portfolio clearly is substandard.

✓ **Academic staff review and sign-off after the assessment is completed**

It is good practice to have an academic staff member review the assessment prior to returning the feedback and portfolio to the student. Often times, there is a sign-off by an academic director or dean. Academic leadership may also institute a quality control spot check of portfolios to ensure consistency in assessment as well as also ensuring all of the approved portfolios meet institutional standards for credit awards.

✓ **Use of faculty-developed rubrics for all assessments**

Best practices dictate that assessors should use a rubric. This rubric should be known to the student so that the student can self-assess every step along the way to submitting the portfolio for assessment. This takes the mystery out of portfolio assessment for both the students and the faculty assessors. When students can see how they have performed in the various rubric categories, such as addressing learning outcomes, using experiences as examples while focusing on the learning from the experiences, demonstrating reflection, and writing at the college level, the learning continues even when the student gets back the assessment. The assessor's feedback provides more learning opportunities for the student, provoking further thought.

✓ Inter-rater reliability studies

Conducting inter-rater reliability studies is an important component of assuring quality in portfolio assessments. These studies can be conducted while providing professional development for faculty. Testing the rubrics to ensure consistency is as important to faculty as it is to students. There are a couple of ways to conduct the studies.

1. As faculty are trained to be assessors, provide sample portfolios for all to assess individually using the same rubric. Once completed, ask faculty to share the results and the insights they gained from the student's portfolio. Good training and solid rubric should result in rubric scores being the same or within a few points of each other. If there is great variability, faculty should discuss the variances and determine if the rubric needs to be changed. Repeat the exercise.

2. Pull random completed and assessed portfolios and assign them to different assessors. Determine if the second assessment is on par with the first assessment. This quality check should be completed at least once per year.

✓ Ongoing professional development for all faculty and staff who are talking to students about prior learning assessment, particularly portfolio assessment

Faculty members must be trained to successfully assess portfolios. Without training or professional development, there is a risk of the assessor expecting the portfolio to be at an "A" grade or to consider inputs rather than outcomes. Staff should also be trained in how to talk about portfolio assessment, identify good candidates, and how to initiate the process for students.

✓ Archiving portfolios

Make sure your portfolios are archived and part of your institutional records retention program. Digital portfolios are easily archived, while hard copy paper portfolios will require storage space and/or duplication.

✓ Plagiarism detection service

Portfolios can easily be registered through turnitin.com or other plagiarism detection services. Ongoing diligence is an important aspect of a good portfolio assessment program. Not only do you not want students to plagiarize, but you also want to make sure portfolios are not sold on the Internet.

✓ Published policies and procedures for portfolio assessment

Transparency is the best insurance for quality. Publish all policies, procedures, and pertinent information about portfolio assessment. Faculty and academic leadership should receive regular updates on portfolio assessment success rates, academic outcomes for students who have earned portfolio credits, how portfolio credits fulfill degree program requirements, and the results of any inter-rater reliability studies.

"Critics of portfolio assessment often cite "giving away credit hours" as their reason for not supporting it. Sharing information, publicizing portfolio assessment policies and procedures, adhering to quality standards, and providing professional development will quiet the critics. In fact, generally speaking, critics are most concerned with making sure students receive a quality postsecondary experience. When critics take a closer look at the rigor of portfolio assessment and the checks and balances in place for excellent oversight, they tend to become convinced that it is an important academic process."

From the Experts

Tina Grant, Executive Director

Center for the Assessment of Post-traditional Instruction, Training, and Learning (CAPITAL)

Excelsior College, Albany, NY

Some academicians are skeptical of the level of rigor required in the portfolio development and assessment process. Much of that skepticism comes from ignorance of the process and can possibly be mitigated by a paradigm shift: simply ask faculty or administrators to take a half hour to write down everything they know, figure out how they know it, describe where they learned it, and demonstrate their application of that knowledge with tangible evidence. The first two minutes of that exercise should provide enough angst to relay the message that the metacognition necessary to describe (let alone substantiate!) one's learning requires a high level of rigor and a wrestling with writing not often required in our most challenging college courses.

Most faculty would agree, then, that such rigor and wrestling with one's own learning is an invaluable exercise, but what may not be as evident is the fact that PLA is beneficial to the institution as well. As Confucius told us, "To know what you know and to know what you do not know…that is true knowledge." Prior learning assessment, then, can help empower learners to own what they know and do well, and just as importantly, it can also help learners of any age identify their own gaps in knowledge. Those gaps can be met through coursework offered by the institution; hence, the CAEL findings that earned credit for prior learning results in increased persistence and completion rates. PLA credit is hard-earned and seems likely to provide the motivation students need to complete. Imagine the motivation and interest the PLA student might have after identifying the courses that will help bridge his or her knowledge gaps and bring degree completion within grasp. Tanya, an employee of CAPITAL at Excelsior College, provides a wonderful example:

> After meeting with her mentor, Tanya, a working mother of three in her mid-thirties, used her PLA experience to design her entire degree program. She submitted two successful portfolios, gaining three credits for process re-engineering and eight credits for family law and litigation. As a result of being able to articulate her knowledge and skills in research, law, and analysis, Tanya then decided to change her original course of study from forensic accounting to public policy. By understanding what she already knew, she could identify which courses she needed to pursue to round out her knowledge and skills, namely public and social policy courses. She knew she would be successful in those courses, because the PLA process allowed her to accurately assess her strengths. After transferring her associate's degree credit and attaining additional PLA credit, Tanya was able to complete a bachelor's degree as a part-time working adult in just two years, earning a 3.7 grade point average. She now uses her degree to help working adults earn credit for their workplace training programs.

It seems that, much like the student who undergoes a portfolio assessment, PLA itself is finally enjoying its own hard-earned time in the spotlight. As institutions move toward recognizing the value of substantiated life and work experience, the nation will move closer to its completion goals, and skeptics of PLA will be hard pressed in their defense against this important, rigorous, life-changing process.

The Important Role of the Assessor

Beyond scoring a portfolio with a rubric, the assessor's evaluation includes all of the following responsibilities:

Determine Legitimacy of the Request for Credit **Note:** *For many portfolio assessment programs, a PLA director/coordinator will check to make sure the portfolio is worthy of an assessment before it is given to an assessor.*	1. Check course description and learning objectives/outcomes and competencies. 2. Check for statement of authenticity and/or whether the portfolio has been checked for plagiarism (turnitin.com). 3. Check documents and artifacts.
Assess the Portfolio	**<u>Use a Rubric</u>** Use the performance standards on the rubric as your guide for determining if all of the course outcomes/objectives have been addressed satisfactorily. Does the student describe learning from experience, as opposed to just the experience itself? Is the learning at the college level? Has the student demonstrated reflection in her/his writing? Has the student linked theory to practice? Has the student shown how the learning might be applied in new situations?
Check the Quality of the Writing	Depending upon your rubric and the values your faculty has determined, is the writing at college level? Has the student used the APA style or other institutionally-preferred academic style and citations as appropriate? Has the student linked her or his evidence to her or his learning claims?
Review of the Documentation	Is the evidence provided sufficient? Does it make sense? Are the artifacts useful and legitimate?
Score the Rubric	Has the student done well enough to be awarded credit? Should credit be awarded or denied? Generally, no partial credit is awarded. For competency-based portfolios, credit may be earned for certain competencies, while other competencies might not have been demonstrated. In this case, students will earn credit for the competencies achieved and work with their academic department to attain the remaining competencies. This philosophy is the foundation for direct assessment competency programs.
Written Feedback	Provide both positive and critical written feedback that provides another mechanism for the student to continue to learn. Keep the tone neutral or positive.
"Close but Not Quite There" Assessments	Is the portfolio good enough that credit can be awarded with a slight revision? If so, are you willing to give the student the feedback and review the portfolio again after the student has made revisions? Occasionally, a student just slightly misses the mark. When a student is really close to the credit award, an excellent assessor will tell the student what needs to be done (sometimes it's as simple as adding another piece of documentation), so the student gains the opportunity to re-submit the portfolio.
Final Review	Determine if credit is awarded or denied.

From the Experts

A Faculty Member's Perspective on Portfolios and Assessment—Melissa Nemon, PhD

Since 2012, I have had the distinct pleasure of teaching courses on prior learning assessment as well as assessing portfolios for a variety of students from all walks of life. I have seen the skilled military professional apply their Military Occupation Specialty (MOS) into a portfolio to move through their educational program more efficiently, thus maximizing their GI Bill. I have read portfolios from wonderful individuals who are going back to school to advance their careers and who carry a wealth of practical knowledge that they can apply to course learning. And I have reviewed numerous portfolios from individuals who recognize that their applied knowledge and expertise—when combined with an understanding of foundational concepts—can help them move past lower level courses more quickly and into courses that more appropriately fit them.

It's not hard to see that I am an advocate of prior learning assessment. It allows students, particularly adult students, the opportunity to move through their program more efficiently while simultaneously reducing education costs and acknowledging that some education is acquired through non-academic sources. But beyond those reasons, prior learning assessments also provide an opportunity for students to gain more control over their education, and this is no small thing. Through PLA, students can move into courses that more accurately fit their learning level, thus, keeping them engaged and ultimately more likely to complete their education.

As an assessor, I am often asked what types of students utilize PLA and, to be honest, it's as wide and varied as any classroom. I have military and veteran students; foreign students; nontraditional students, including those returning to college after long absences; professionals looking to advance their careers; Peace Corps and AmeriCorps members; and even retired individuals who are looking to go into a second career or pursue a lifelong dream of acquiring a degree. There is no single type of PLA student in the same way there is no "type" of successful college student. In fact, the single best deciding factor of who is a good candidate for PLA is the individual who can expertly connect their professional experience directly to specific course outcomes and expectations.

Don't get me wrong, I was not always an advocate of PLA. I had heard about it in passing when I was an associate dean at a small private university, and I mostly had heard others complain about the idea of it. I mean, how can we reasonably measure someone's prior experiences and align them with course outcomes? I've heard many academics lament the idea of PLA, believing that it was just code speak for watering down the degree or simply moving people through the system. But it wasn't until I started to look into the PLA process and system itself that I began to see the high rates of rigor and integrity involved in the process.

Let's be clear, PLA is not a subjective process. Students create a portfolio on a specific course. This is no small feat, as some of these portfolios can run upwards of 40 pages. So how do they create these portfolios? Well, the first step is get their hands on the course outcomes (often found in the most recent syllabus on file or they are held by the academic department). Then students write a full portfolio focusing on the required course outcomes by combining their personal, professional, and academic experiences with research and information on the topic. They express fundamental knowledge of terminology and definitions and tease that apart with examples, observations, reflections, abstract conceptualization, and active experimentation. They have to fully cover the entirety of the course and demonstrate equivalent proficiency as if they had sat through a 16-week course. If this sounds difficult—it is. Picture writing a single paper that encompasses everything you need to cover in an entire course and you get an idea of what these students are doing.

Continued on next page.

Then the portfolio is turned in to a faculty assessor in the field. The reviewer has to examine the syllabus, the portfolio, and any supporting documentation that students provide to back-up their assertions of proficiency or experience. In short, assessors are looking for students to prove their knowledge through expressions of learning behavior by explaining how they derive meaning from specific experiences, exploring how they learned what they now know and how they continue to use it, and by expressing how they value learning.

The review process alone can take about two to three hours in total; and at the end, assessors typically fill out a rubric to ensure that there is consistency in the course reviewing and rating. As a result the whole process has ensured validity through standardized scoring and rating. And this is why academically established course outcomes are so critical because the more concrete the course outcomes are in the syllabus, the more directly a correlation between experience and course expectations can be determined. By connecting PLA to the expectations of the course, we can reduce bias and increase reliability in assessment and review. In the same way many academics tie specific assignments directly to course outcomes, the PLA is tied back to all course outcomes.

You might be thinking that not all academics agree on how to teach a course, and you are 100 percent correct. But the methodology by which one teaches a course does not necessarily stray from the course outcomes. Most academics who teach a course on sociology are going to ensure that they cover the three core theories of functionalism, symbolic interactionism, and conflict theory. How they teach it or cover it in class might be different, but the fact that they still cover it is mandatory. To pass sociology, you should know these three theories—that's an expected outcome—and in my experience, I have yet to see a sociology syllabus without some version of this outcome.

Reviewers are not that different (and that's not surprising considering we are all academics). For those of us who review PLA portfolios, we all read the course outcomes carefully and understand that those must be achieved first and foremost. As a result, in my four years of reviewing experience I have never overturned an existing score based on an appeal request. In fact, out of all the times that I have been asked to review a portfolio on appeal, my score has never been more than a point apart from the original score, which speaks to the lack of bias in the syllabus outcomes and the reliability of the assessment rubric.

In my experience teaching, I have seen a variety of students who come to class with incredible life experiences and practical knowledge that supplement their learning in my classroom. I would argue that, in many cases, most academics see these students and often work with them to ensure that their existing knowledge can be combined with the class lessons. This is why PLA is not only a great tool for students but also a natural extension of the academic process. PLA is like the instructor or professor who helps the student connect academic proficiency with practical knowledge. PLA is the tool that allows students to explore what they know in a more meaningful and academic way, providing direction and foundational concepts to connect what they know to how they know it. In the end, PLA is a mechanism to help more students easily move through their education, retain their desire and drive to stay in school, and ultimately complete their degree. Which, let's face it, isn't that why we are in education in the first place?

Student Portfolio Example #4—Andrea

Here is another portfolio example. As you read this portfolio, consider the following:

1. Does the student's introduction aid in understanding her reason for writing the portfolio? Does it set a context for assessment?
2. Does the student differentiate between what she does and what she learns?

3. Does the student write at the college level?

4. Does the student make the case for credit for this course?

This portfolio is for LEAD 310— Leadership Theory & Practice II

Andrea's Portfolio[10]

Introduction

Andrea sets the context for her portfolio with a little background information and some personal details. This gives the assessor a mental picture of sorts.

I am a 30-year-old mother of two beautiful little girls and wife of a high school football coach. I have always been around sports growing up and continue my passion for athletics in my current profession as an athletic coach in public education. I have also been fortunate enough to be able to continue my love of nursing as a district school nurse. I have always thought that my experience in sports enabled me to become a great leader. Whether it is personal or career oriented, I have always had the natural ability to lead. During the process of writing my learning autobiography, I learned that my introduction to leadership started on the softball field. After high school, I was awarded a scholarship to play softball for a well-known university. I believe that I was awarded a scholarship not only because of my athletic skills but also my ability to lead. After a few years on the field, I decided that my life needed to take another path and chose to attend nursing school. I had always wanted to have a profession in the medical field, and I could not think of a more perfect career for someone that is self-driven, hardworking, and eager to learn. I loved the autonomy of nursing and the ability to positively impact someone's life on a daily basis.

During my time at the ABC community college I maintained a high GPA, graduated at the top of my class, planned and organized our pinning ceremony, and was chosen to complete my internship in the surgical intensive care unit of the local hospital. After graduation, I was selected to be in the Graduate Nurse program at ABC Regional Medical Center where I continued to work as a registered nurse for six years. I started out on the Intermediate Care Unit as a bedside nurse, but was quickly promoted to unit supervisor in one year. Largely due to my abilities as a smart and competent nurse but also because of my ability to positively influence others, take on more responsibilities, and attempt to change the culture of the unit. As a bedside nurse, I joined the Unit Based Council and created a mission statement and core values for our unit. After a few years on the Intermediate Care Unit, I was promoted to nurse manager over two medical—surgical units and an observation unit. I really grew in that role, in regards to leadership, largely because I had a great mentor in my director (see Documents 1 and 2). I use strategies and skills learned during my two years as nurse manager on a daily basis in my new career as school nurse and high school athletic coach.

In this learning portfolio, I will be discussing my experiences and how they pertain to the leadership course **Leadership Theory and Practice II, Lead 310**. This is a 3 semester credit hour course.

Course Description: *"This course is an introduction to leadership theory and practice. Students will develop an understanding of the behaviors and characteristics of leaders through examination of current leadership models. Course objectives include; defining the nature of leadership and the attributes of a leader through a study of current leadership theories, developing an understanding of the communication and interpersonal processes necessary to lead effectively, developing an understanding of the moral dimensions of leadership by exploring the areas of ethics and personal*

---

[10] Used with permission from the author of this portfolio.

integrity, gaining an awareness of the impact of gender, race and cultural issues in the development of leaders and leadership theory, and lastly developing an understanding of the potential of leadership to transform individuals, organizations, and society."

In this narrative, I will discuss the leadership attributes that I possess, my knowledge of interpersonal communication and how it relates to effective leadership, my experience as a strong female leader as it relates to gender issues in leadership, and lastly I will discuss my experience and knowledge as a leader and how leadership can change individuals, organizations, and society. I have always felt that I am a strong willed natural leader with the ability to influence those around me. I was able to use my skills and abilities to climb the career ladder from bedside nurse to nurse manager in three years, and with the help of my director/mentor we were able to change the culture of our units and turn them into highly functioning satisfactory places to work. In preparation for this course, I admit that I do not have much experience with gender or race issues in leadership. The majority of my experience was gained in the nursing field, which is predominantly run by women.

Objective #1: Define the nature of leadership and the attributes of a leader through a study of current theories.

As I mentioned in the introduction, I learned about leadership on the softball field. Unfortunately, the leadership tactics I was introduced to in college were negative, fearful, and manipulative. I knew from making through those couple of years that when my opportunity came to lead, that I would do it differently. Upon entering the workforce, I was fortunate enough to work for a director that was held in high regard with staff for her knowledge and work ethic. Although she was well respected, she lacked support with staff on administrative issues. Even though I was a recently graduated nurse, she allowed me the opportunity to participate on the Unit Based Council where I created a mission statement and core values for our unit (see Document 3). Along with participating on unit committees, I was selected to take the lead on improving our Hospital Consumer Assessment of Healthcare Providers and Systems (HCAHPS) scores. I compiled information from the *HCAHPS Handbook* (Studer, Robinson, and Cook 2010) and created a PowerPoint presentation discussing courtesy and respect (see Document 4), the category our unit was scoring lowest in, and presented to the entire staff during staff meetings and was approached by administration to present during our house wide nurse meetings.

> Notice that this narrative so far describes experiences without referencing the learning derived from them or evidence of reflection at this point.

As I moved up the career ladder, I worked under a boss that encouraged me to explore leadership theories and develop my own style while incorporating my own strong personality traits and general beliefs. I learned through my interactions with different leaders (directors, other managers, and administrators) and took little pieces of their styles as well as those that I read about and incorporated them into my leadership style. I have had numerous leadership roles in my career; unit supervisor, nurse manager, school district registered nurse, athletic coach, and I have found that effective leadership happens when you are able to mold your style and adjust to the audience you are serving. I believe that a successful leader has a strong sense of self, has a vision of where they are going, and a plan to get there. I learned from different experiences that you can adjust your style without changing your overall goal or compromising your personal integrity.

> Here the student references leadership theory. She links her experiences to learning in the next paragraph.

In preparation for my career in nursing leadership I was introduced to the book *The 360 Degree Leader* by John Maxwell. In this book he discusses the Five Levels of Leadership and during my time at ABC Regional Medical Center I found myself working through these levels. In the first level, Position, he discusses the fact that people will follow you because they have to, because of your position and that in order to move up the levels, a good leader will find ways to influence those around them and build relationships so that people will follow you because they want to, which is the next level of leadership, Permission. Successful leaders are always improving and growing. The next level, Production, discusses the theory that people will follow you because of what you have done for the organization. I believe some leaders get stagnant in this position. There is a feeling of success attached to this level; people are appreciative of your work, it is fun, and a lot gets accomplished. The fourth level, People Development, is essential to effective leadership since these people are following you because of what you have done for them. This level is all about leadership production, putting value and stock into the employees; growing and mentoring new leaders. The final level of leadership is Personhood, where people follow you because of who are and what you represent. Maxwell (2005) states that this level of leadership is out of personal control and is up to the people that you have led for a long period of time to put you there.

With my new career in the public school system I have learned that it is important for me to draw closer to the leaders that display positive leadership characteristics, take the time to develop people, have a clear vision and goal for the future. In order for me to grow in leadership in my new field of high school coaching, I need to have positive role models with characteristics that I can emulate. During difficult conversations with student athletes about playing time, practice effort, and general attitudes, I have been able to incorporate lessons from watching my athletic director handle these situations as well as from my time as manager observing and participating with my director during times of critical conversations with employees.

Objective #2: Develop an understanding of the communication and interpersonal processes necessary to lead effectively.

During my first few weeks as a nurse manager, I needed to discuss a core measure fallout with a staff member. Core measures are different regulations the government put in place as best practices for patients, and all issues must be addressed prior to discharge or the hospital is at risk for not being fully reimbursed for the care given. Usually these issues could be fixed in house prior to the patient being discharged, and they were little fixes that were just a lack of attention to detail. My approach was a straightforward matter of fact confrontation while sitting out at the nurses' station. My first interaction with this employee and I proceeded to explain what the error was, how I believe that it was made, the process she needed to complete in order to fix the problem, and that these types of errors were not going to be tolerated. I ended up offending some staff members and coming off rude and with a kind of a know-it-all attitude. Although my statements were correct, that was not the image I wanted my employees to have of me.

Here the student shows evidence of reflection, learning from her experience.

My early experience as a new nurse manager unearthed my lack of knowledge about cultivating relationships with my employees and understanding communication styles. I learned through different conflicts and crises that I had to adapt and change my communication style to meet the certain situation or person I was dealing with. I was not aware of the impact my words could have on employees.

I learned from observing my director during performance counseling with employees and through my attendance at a workshop entitled Crucial Conversations about interpersonal communication and developing employees. In the book *Crucial Conversations*, it is discussed that these types of conversations occur when there are opposing opinions, strong emotions, and the stakes are high. In nursing, there are always high stakes and strong emotions, and in order to obtain a working relationship and ensure that both sides feel heard and validated, trust must be established (Grenny, et al. 2012.) In order to lead successfully, time and energy must be put forth in development of people. Maxwell (2005) discusses the difference between equipping people versus developing them. The concept of equipping someone is teaching them how to do a job, run a machine, about departmental procedures, etc. Developing people takes time, effort, and patience. One theory of staff development follows an eight step process starting with taking the time and committing to long term development, discovering employee dreams and desires, leading everyone differently, using organizational goals for individual development, helping them discover themselves, being willing and ready to have difficult conversations, celebrating the right wins, and preparing them for leadership (Maxwell 2005.)

I have applied these processes and communication techniques in my nursing career by developing a communication tool for the day and night shifts to use to pass on important information discussed during the morning supervisors' meeting. In this meeting, new patients with core measure issues are discussed, assignments are made for patients waiting in the ER, and staffing decisions are made. On my unit there were disgruntled staff members on both shifts due to the lack of communication about core measures and staffing. After a few close calls on core measure fall outs and discussions with disgruntled shift supervisors about staffing, I decided to develop a communication tool to be used by the unit supervisors to aide in communication between shifts (see Document 5). I have also applied these techniques in my new position in public education when dealing with administrators, parents, coworkers, and students alike. I am much more mindful and intentional with my communication as well as more observant of other's language cues. In order to have effective change, trust must be established with employees, time must be spent getting to know the true issues, and development up the ranks is essential.

Objective #3: Develop an understanding of the moral dimensions of leadership by exploring the areas of ethics and personal integrity.

As a manager, I was responsible for supporting certain policies, protocols, or initiatives for my staff and units. One initiative my staff and I were not completely excited about was the implementation of sitter cameras on our unit. I understood the necessity and purpose but I also had to take into consideration my staff's hesitancy on the program (increased work load, increased volume of pts, etc.). I needed to find a happy medium where I could still present the idea and stand behind the goal while also being empathetic to my staff and listening to and addressing their concerns. I needed to push the project through without compromising my personal integrity. I did voice my concerns with my director and the CNO through meetings and conferences about increased workloads and the fear of the increased patient volume. Ultimately, the project was approved and implemented with patient guidelines and increased staffing grids.

Since I was able to effectively communicate the concerns of the unit to administration, a criteria was developed and daily checks put in place in order to ensure the cameras were being used for appropriate patients and that the staff felt validated and they were being protected as well. I learned from this experience that I was able to be a voice and a leader for my unit without having to compromise on my integrity. I was able to effectively lead from the middle, a concept discussed in the book *360 Degree Leader* by John Maxwell.

Simon Sinek, author of *Leaders Eat Last* (2014), discusses the concept of integrity and how it builds trust with employees. Employees need to know that information being presented—good, bad, indifferent—is the truth and that the direction is good for all and not just the leader. I also utilized Maxwell's concept of leading from the middle when dealing with this particular situation. Tensions are high when leading from the middle; balancing authority and power of position, initiating without overstepping, assessing the environment of current leadership, assessment of your job, and living without the appreciation of staff (Maxwell 2005.)

In my current position in public education, I have been in situations dealing with young athletes and other coaches and find myself struggling with the concept of loyalty without compromising personal integrity. It is easier to discuss a difficult plan when you have integrity on your side. Integrity is a leadership attribute that has to be proven before it can be effective.

Objective #4: Develop an understanding of the potential of leadership to transform individuals, organizations, and society.

During my time as a registered nurse at ABC Regional Medical Center, I was a member of the Unit Based Council for the intermediate care unit. One of the frustrations of the staff was the nurse to patient ratio. The staff felt as though the acuity of the patients put the nurses at risk with a ratio of 5:1. My role was to take the concerns of the staff and present to the Board of Trustees a proposal to decrease the patient ratio of 5:1 to 3-4:1. Over a period of several months, I conducted unit research as well as national research, staff interviews, and worked with another staff member to develop our proposal. When our time came to present to the board, we had strong data to back up our claim and proposal that the ratio needed to be lowered in order to improve patient safety and satisfaction as well as increase staff satisfaction, tenure, and decrease workload (see Document 6).

Throughout this process, many staff members were discouraging saying that it had been attempted in the past and nothing ever came of it. This motivated me even more to work hard and get results for my coworkers. I knew that in the past there was not as much information and data to substantiate claims about staffing ratios, and I knew that if I had a strong presentation filled with emotion and facts that I could influence the board to hear our story.

Here the student links theory to her experience.

John Maxwell's theory of leading up from within an organization is displayed in the previous example. Leading people from beyond your position is a challenge and requires a great deal of influence. Leadership is not only about position but about the ability to influence those around you, to have people follow because of who you are and what you have done regardless of your rank in the organization. Leading up means that you are willing to take the tough jobs, pay your dues, work in the shadows of the those above you, put your thoughts and ideas on the line, admit faults without offering excuses, go above and beyond the role, always be willing to volunteer and help, perform tasks that are not necessarily part of your job, and take responsibilities for your responsibilities (Maxwell 2005).

As my career has moved from hospital nursing to management to public education, I have learned that no matter what avenue my career takes me there is always the opportunity to lead. Leading up by being an example for those above me; athletic director, administrators, principals, etc. Leading across: other coaches, teachers, school nurses, etc., by displaying integrity and a clear vision for the future while spending the time to develop those around me. Leading Down with students, athletes and community.

Conclusion

Throughout my career in nursing and now in public education, I believe that these experiences have prepared me to be a role model and an example of positive leadership. I learned many lessons about leadership attributes and styles. Those I want to incorporate into my own style and those that I recognize to steer clear of. I have learned through trial and error in different aspects of my professional career the importance of communication and developing interpersonal relationships in order to create effective leadership. I have experienced firsthand the effects of the potential of leadership and how it can change an organization and individuals through my work at ABC Regional Medical Center. I plan to continue leadership work as my career unfolds in public education.

Hopefully, in the coming years I will be able to introduce and teach young high school students the opportunities of health science careers and continue to guide them in their athletic aspirations. I am always looking for new ways to be a more influential person in my work, community, and personal relationships.

References

Grenny, J., McMillan, R., Patterson, K., and Switzler, A. 2012. *Crucial conversations: Tools for talking when stakes are high.* McGraw Hill.

Maxwell, J. 2005. *The 360 [degree symbol] leader: Developing your influence from anywhere in the organization.* Nashville, TN: Nelson Business.

Sinek, S. 2014. *Leaders eat last: Why some teams pull together and others don't.* New York, NY: The Penguin Group.

Studer, Q., Robinson, B.C., and Cook, K. 2010. *The HCAHPS handbook: Hardwire your hospital for pay-for-performance success.* Gulf Breeze, FL: Fire Starter Publishing.

Andrea's Supporting Documentation Included

- The "Daily Huddle" Communication Tool she designed
- Courtesy and Respect Presentation that Andrea wrote and presented at staff meetings
- Vision Statement and Core Values Andrea wrote for her unit
- The PowerPoint presentation she designed to show the data as to why the patient/nurse ratio should be lower
- Performance Appraisal with these evaluator comments:

  > "Andrea has recently transferred from a clinical role to a leadership role in the last couple of months; her prior supervisor states she is an expert clinician and resource to staff. She has been consistent in managing their performance, and she frequently performs as a coach and mentor. She is well balanced, has a strong sense of responsibility, displays integrity, and strives to do her best. She has taken on several projects and has proven to get results, be very helpful, follows directions and instructions well, and to be flexible. I feel Andrea will be a strong asset to the nursing leadership team."

  > "Areas for improvement: Continue her educational and professional development; development of vision and forethought for her departments; develop fiscal knowledge and accountability."

- Letter of Verification

ABC Regional Medical Center Letterhead

November 19, 2014

Dear Portfolio Evaluator,

This letter testifies that Andrea was employed at ABC Regional Medical Center on a full-time basis as a nurse manager from Nov. 2011 – Aug. 2013. I was director over the units that she managed and hired her to work under me. Andrea managed two medical surgical departments and an observation department.

During her time as my nurse manager, Andrea used her leadership skills on numerous occasions. I hired Andrea as my nurse manager after she excelled in a prior position as a charge nurse. Andrea was a self-motivated participative leader that possessed critical thinking, great time management skills, and was detail oriented. She worked diligently to learn the behaviors of her employees so she could communicate and lead more effectively. Andrea also worked closely with administration on implementation of new projects for the unit and was able to garner support from the staff for these sometimes unpopular initiatives. She took the lead in presentations to our unit staff as well as house-wide meetings. Andrea performed at an above average level to her peers and was able to aide in the positive change in the culture of our units. She grew into her own leadership style as the years progressed and was well respected by employees, peers, and administration. The leadership skills Andrea already possessed coupled with the skills learned during her time as nurse manager should enable her to be successful in future endeavors.

Andrea was a dynamic part of developing a great team of caregivers. She will be missed, and we wish her all the best with her educational and professional goals.

Sincerely,

Signature Here

Name Here, RN, BSN

Director of Medical/Surgical Observation

Andrea's Assessor Feedback

Andrea's Portfolio Assessment (Leadership Theory & Practice II)

Rubric Score: 20 out of 28

RUBRIC SCORES

Course Outcomes Identified and Addressed	3/4
Learning from Experience	3/4
Understanding of Theory and Practice	3/4
Reflection	3/4
Learning Application	3/4
Communication	3/4
Supporting Documentation	2/4

ASSESSOR WRITTEN FEEDBACK

Through this fairly wordy narrative, the applicant did address the course description and the course objectives and did tie in her experience to every learning outcome. The communication style needs attention in grammar and syntax and the supporting documentation could have used additional professional "external" verification. There is no doubt that this applicant has the experience and knowledge. This assessor would have also encouraged more focus on leadership in diverse environments.

Andrea's score was sufficient to earn her full credit for her portfolio. A point lower would have meant credit denial.

Here is an example of a portfolio that achieved the highest possible score for credit.[11]

Student Portfolio Example #5—Michael

Course Title: PAD-332 Municipal Government Operations

Course Description

This course will examine the functions, hierarchy, and management of various local government departments. Students will learn the interrelationships of various community departments as well as the roles of leadership and community boards within local government.

Course Learning Objectives or Outcomes for PAD 332 Municipal Government Operations:

- Identify the potential constraints and benefits of various types of municipal governance
- Assess the functions and structure of municipal governments for their impact on local services
- Examine the relationships between the responsibilities of financial officers and the fiscal challenges facing local governments
- Articulate the effects of active citizen involvement within the government using appropriate evidence
- Construct potential solutions for the economic challenges facing municipalities that effectively address all relevant factors

---

Michael's Portfolio

Introduction

Greetings, my name is Michael. I am 44 years old, grew up, and live in a small town in Maine. I have been married to my wife for the past 20 years, and we have raised two daughters now at the ages of 21 and 16. I attended the University of Southern Maine and Central Maine Community College attaining an Associate of Applied Science degree in Business Administration and Management.

By nature, I am a hardworking person with a strong work ethic. I obtained my first job at the age of 10 delivering morning newspapers six days a week, and continued to do so until I entered high school. I have been working a job, in most cases two or three at the same time, ever since.

Currently I am the town manager, a part-time emergency medical dispatcher for a local ambulance service, and an adjunct instructor in the business department at a community college. I am a soft spoken and kind individual who achieves an immense amount of satisfaction by helping others. This has been a lifelong trait that has earned me the respect and admiration of my family, friends, and citizens in the community in which I live. I have been working for the town for the past 23 years.

> Clearly, Michael has direct government experience. He presents an excellent introduction to set the context for his portfolio.

I began my tenure with the town as a firefighter/emergency medical technician in December of 1990. Since then, I have held many positions of rank within the department including fire inspector, instructor, and Deputy Fire Chief. In 2003, I was appointed as the

---

[11] This portfolio was used with the permission of its author.

Assistant Town Manager. This afforded me the opportunity to meet and correspond with other municipal managers, attend trainings and conferences for professional managers, and begin to make executive decisions and draft policy. In January 2006, the Town Council appointed me as the interim Town Manager. I am happy to say that based on my prior work history with the town and an endorsing recommendation from the outgoing manager, I was appointed full-time in June of that year without the Council performing a candidate search.

Learning Narrative

Objective #1: Identify the potential constraints and benefits of various types of municipal governance.

I have been employed as the chief executive officer in my town for almost eight years (see Documents 1, 2, and 3—Employment Contracts). Gained with my experience, I have firsthand knowledge of the five-forms of governance for the nearly 500 cities and towns in the State of Maine (Haag, 1993). They are identified as Council/Manager, Town meeting/Council/Manager, Town meeting/Selectmen/Manager, Town meeting/Selectman/Administrative Assistant, and Mayor/Council/Administrator. My town, by charter, is governed by a Town meeting/Council/Manager form of government. Our form of government uses the oldest form of democracy in the United States, which allows for local citizens to be directly involved with public policy decisions. Citizens are called together annually for a town meeting at which time a proposed municipal budget is presented and voted on, each line item at a time. When the budget is passed, the taxes are committed for the next year, and the budget is administered by the town manager with oversight from the Town Council. The manager is the chief executive officer and oversees the day-to-day operation of all municipal departments. In all of these models, the selectmen or councilors are elected and are the legislative body for their entity.

As a manager, I frequently meet and consult with other municipal leaders and/or elected officials for collaborative efforts, trainings, shared issues, and common interests. I belong to several professional management associations that provide an opportunity for such meetings but I have also met individually with community leaders, as well. I have experienced both the constraints and benefits of each form of government.

Examining the Selectman/Administrator models, I have witnessed some of the constraints by observing other community's public meetings. One of the major limitations is timely decision making. In a community that does not have a professional manager, business meetings are conducted one to two times each month. It is the responsibility of the elected officials to come together and sign municipal pay warrants, conduct public hearings for new proposed policy, review general assistance cases, and discuss daily operations. Decisions are sometimes held up by the time it takes for these officials to meet.

To illustrate an example, while trying to negotiate shared services agreements for our public works and emergency medical services (see Documents 4 and 5—Shared Services Contracts), it was necessary for me to meet with our neighboring community's town manager. Their form of governance is the Town Meeting/Selectman/Manager. This requires their manager to bring any negotiations to the Selectmen for their consideration. Their manager does not have the ability to enter into agreements on the municipality's behalf without their authorization. In my community, our governance structure allows for the manager to enter into contractual agreements and then advise the Council of such action. A benefit of having a Council/Manger allows for the municipality to react more quickly and provide for greater efficiency.

To compare these forms of governance further, there are two cities within 10 miles of our town that have the Mayor/Council/Administrator form. These are the largest communities in our county, and their activity is prevalent in the press offering ongoing comparison with other government styles. In most nationwide models, a Mayor is the chief executive officer who, through appointed department heads, directs municipal operations. In Maine, the day-to-day operations are usually managed by hired administrators. The mayors are figureheads and in some cases are only a public representation for their community. Recalling conversations with former mayors, they have indicated their lack of decision making power. They do have minimal voting power and are often used to break tie votes when a Council reaches an impasse. The mayors are elected officials and their personal agendas, often the promises made during a campaign, sometimes are the forefront of policy proposals made during their tenure.

A common disadvantage that sometimes troubles communities is that Selectmen and Councilors are elected officials. I have worked with folks, who have been elected, with little or no experience in municipal government operations. Some will run for office with the mindset that they can make widespread changes towards their beliefs. I experienced this very situation in July of 2003. A gentleman who was elected to our Council had intentions to "crash and thrash" by making staffing cuts, reduce spending, and reduce taxes. Over time, I refined him to a point that eventually turned his motivations in the opposite direction. When his term expired, after nine years, he walked away admitting that he had a whole new outlook and understanding of why things were done the way they were. His attitude became more supportive than destructive.

The student does a nice job of demonstrating critical thinking and reflection in comparing different government structures. He is also able to distinguish his learning from his experiences.

The benefit of some of these forms of government is a person who remains constant. An executive officer, such as a manager, administrator, or administrative assistant is appointed, not elected. They, therefore, have a longer-term, historical knowledge of the community's operations. Being one of these people, I have had the chance to experience Councilors who have come and gone. I have had to spend significant amounts of time teaching each of these individuals with meetings, reports, other documentation, and sometimes casual one-on-one conversation.

I have functioned with all of the forms of leadership in each of the communities around us. I have served on a regional school consolidation committee, a regional public safety answering point/ emergency dispatching committee, and currently serve on a legislative policy committee (Maine Municipal Association 2013), regional council of governments, and regional rail coalition group (see Documents 6, 7, 8 and 9—Documents of Committee participation).

I have learned to respect each community's governance choice by understanding the operational and political differences. They have chosen their form based on population, dynamic needs, local economic factors, and popular vote.

Objective #2: Assess the functions and structure of municipal governments for their impact on local services.

Regardless of the local governance structure, organized municipalities are tasked with servicing the population within their boundaries with a comprehensive range of amenities. However, each of those entities may differ slightly in how those services are administered and delivered.

A community has an authorized person to monitor the daily activity of municipal operations. These officials may be elected or appointed. Organizations follow a chain of command system that differs from town to town, but all have the elected officials at the top of the hierarchy. Below the elected officials, are the separate departments that are categorized by function. These departments are largely administrative services, police, fire, public works, assessing, library, planning, health, welfare, solid waste, and parks and recreation.

In our community, department heads are appointed by me and answer directly to me. They all received their guidance and management through a central office. Using the management by objectives theory (Luthra 2013), I work with my staff and stay in regular, weekly communication. Exchanging information with each department head allows for a team approach to operations and results in cooperation and proficiency. We base our objectives by goal setting and reviewing those goals during an annual review.

In other communities, the executive officer may only be in charge of just some of the department heads. It is not uncommon to see elected fire chiefs, road commissioners, town clerks, and treasurers. These folks may report to the local elected legislative body but only answer directly to the voters. When I have examined the shortcomings of having elected departmental officials, a common thread is reduced oversight and accountability. This occasionally leads to misappropriation, violations of laws and regulations, and poor productivity and performance. An elected official does not necessarily mean the official has to be qualified for the position. They may have been elected by popular vote. Voters are not in the best position to monitor actions of that individual to ensure best practices and management. In other cases, I have witnessed elected officials who may be perfectly suited and the best skilled person for a job eliminated because of public opinion, not by measured production.

Every community has some level of public safety by providing it with employees of the municipality, relying on a county or state agency, agreements with a neighboring town, or private contractor. I operate a full-time police department and a fire/rescue department with on call personnel. Towns must provide the archiving of public information, vital records, licensing, and permitting and conducting elections. Services that are optional by local choice are library, parks and recreation, planning and development, public works, and social services. The demographics of the locality usually drive the structure and level of each service. Communities with low populations will not have a large demand for public safety services. Cities with larger populations are likely to have a greater need for social services. Some services are determined at the choice of the elected officials. I know, for example that our neighboring community stresses the need for full-time fire and EMS coverage. Having a response volume of slightly more than double what is required in our town, its need may not be warranted. Their annual budget for the same services is almost six times that of our $84,000, yet their voters have supported and approved at their town meeting. I am not able to defend such a high cost to our taxpayers and, therefore, I employ a smaller sized, more cost efficient fire/rescue.

Each year, when I am drafting my proposed budget, it is critical that I evaluate the level of need for each department. For example, when considering our emergency medical services, I take a look at response histories for the past several years. Although this is not an accurate method of benchmarking due to the unpredictable nature of medical services, I also look at the dynamics of our population. Communities with older populations will place a higher demand on EMS. Taking into consideration that more and more people are using EMS services for nonemergency calls, the trend causes slight increases to this budget annually. An additional example is the necessity for me to analyze our historical usage of salt and sand deployment during the winter months. Predicting how much my public works department will need in the coming year can be hit or miss. It is important to ensure there is an adequate supply on hand.

Objective #3: Examine the relationships between the responsibilities of financial officers and the fiscal challenges facing local governments.

Financial officers in a municipality have a high degree of responsibility that requires flawless accuracy and accountability. In my position, I am ultimately responsible for the financial status of our community as the appointed treasurer (see Document

The student addresses the learning objective directly and succinctly, a hallmark of an excellent portfolio.

10—Record of Sworn Appointment). However, I am not the person who does the daily accounting. Our municipality has a full-time finance director who manages the entire financial bookkeeping. In large towns and cities, it is very common that the chief executive officer is not the same person maintaining the books. In previous trainings (see Documents 11 and 12—Certifications of training/participation), I have learned the importance of having multiple sets of eyes on financial records to inspect for errors and to ensure there is no fraudulent activity.

In comparison between the responsibilities, I create, propose, defend, and obtain approval of an operational budget. I monitor the administration of the budget throughout the year and authorize purchase orders as requested by each department. The finance director, using the funds allocated by the approved budget, receives and records incoming revenues, and creates payment warrants. The payment warrants are reviewed by me, authorized by the Council, and payments are executed. I review the transaction records weekly during meetings with my finance director to reconcile balances of each of our accounts.

The financial challenges, that I face each year, are the increased demand for public services that carry a caveat of no additional funding and reduced revenue sharing from the State. I am tasked, annually, with having to do more with less. To solve some of these issues, I have consolidated positions as they open up by attrition. I have demonstrated that I can provide the same services without having to increase the overall operational costs. To do this in the past year, I reduced capital expenditure budgets to reallocate funds for more pertinent services. I do recognize the potential negative impact that this practice has on future needs. The capital funds are essentially savings accounts for future projects. A particular example that has occurred recently is our need to replace Christmas decorations that are displayed in our downtown during the holiday season. Funding limitations did not allow for the replacement of deteriorating and visually unpleasing adornments. I challenged our public works staff to use their collective talents to fabricate decorations, which are similar to those that can be purchased commercially. They were successful. I also boosted morale by giving a task that was out of their daily routine.

Another fiscal challenge that I will continue to face is revenue generation to augment depleting sources. As the demand for lower taxes prompts the reduction of budgets, establishing fees for services has become a necessary evil. I had to defend an argument that over-users, of a particular service, should have some level of financial ownership. I have implemented certain fees at our transfer station for people who bring trash items that are costly to dispose of. Oversized furniture, for example, brought in whole has a cost to the municipality that is above and beyond what the general tax base covers. Naturally we had resistance with the new fee, and I was faced with another dilemma. I solved this problem after meeting with my transfer station manager and discussing alternatives. We came to the conclusion that if staff were to breakdown the furniture into individual recyclable components, then the material that costs us money to dispose of was drastically minimized.

Objective #4: Articulate the effects of active citizen involvement within the government using appropriate evidence.

Citizen involvement is a critical component of public policy. Depending on the form of governance in any given community, the public may or may not play a role in the adoption of budgets or policy. In our community, I have learned that it is advantageous to include the public when formulating regulations. With a small administrative staff, it is often difficult for us to see all sides of an issue. Including others who may have a unique interest in the issue often brings to the table opinions, ideas, and opportunity for appealing solutions. I spent the better part of two years working with a group of citizens updating our municipal Comprehensive Plan. We were able to bring continuity to the plan by allowing different perspectives and valued input from our population by those participating in the process. Including people gives them ownership in the project, a willingness to defend their project and are more likely to campaign for support. The successful culmination of our plan was successfully adopted locally with validation at the state level (see Document 13—State Approval Letter).

Another instance of citizen involvement was the need to deal with issues created when the State of Maine legalized the sale and use of consumer fireworks. This relaxation of the ban of using fireworks triggered some unruliness expected with any new release from prohibition. Citizen complaints began to pile up with demands for local regulation. I drafted a proposed local ordinance and invited the public for review (see Document 14—Public Meeting Minutes). After a couple meetings with rather heated discussion, a compromise was mostly accepted and submitted for a public referendum. This passed by popular vote at our election in November 2012. By including the public in this process, it showed me that my original proposal would not have been accepted without some modification. Incorporating the resident's suggestions, there was greater suitability.

Inviting citizen involvement has become easier with the development of social media. I post and edit both our municipal webpage and our Facebook page. Our webpage has a feature allowing citizens to sign up to receive direct e-mail notifications of public meeting notices.

Objective #5: Construct potential solutions for the economic challenges facing municipalities that effectively address all relevant factors.

It is my own personal opinion that the demand for increased public services, with limited funding, is a trend that is not going to culminate anytime soon. This situation will continue to get worse before it gets better, and dollars will have to be stretched further.

Small scale, I have had to consider and have implemented minor procedures in energy conservation, such as requiring the use of smart power strips that detect when electronics are not being used and turn off the devices. We have adopted a no idling policy for municipal vehicles in an effort to conserve fuel. Documents are now being created and distributed in electronic format to support the reduced use of paper, and duplication expenses.

On an intermediate scale, merging of services is allowing us to provide the same level of service at reduced cost by sharing personnel and resources. In the last year, I have contracted two of our municipal services with our neighboring community. We share an animal control officer with seven other towns. Contracting public services to the private sector cannot be discounted and is considered periodically. Competitive bidding for services keeps expenses in check with rival providers.

Inter-governmental efforts will have to be contemplated at an even higher level. The joining of communities and sharing administrations will have to be studied. This will be challenging as local control is very near and dear to most voters (ICMA 2012). Countywide services will also have to be explored as an option, as well.

Conclusion

Municipal government operations are much broader than the few objectives set out for this course. In my experience, I have had the ability to learn all aspects of municipal government while serving in various positions of civic hierarchy. Each of these positions has contributed to the lifelong learning that has enabled me to be successful in my job as chief executive today (see Document 15—Reference Letter).

Until now, I have never received formal education specifically for my position. I would like to think that my continued employment as the town manager speaks as reference towards my qualifications. These qualifications have all been accumulated through on-the-job training, informal apprenticeship, cooperative educational opportunities with others in my field, and self-instruction (see Document 16—MTCMA Certification).

I have cultured human resource skills by working alongside my employees every day and using established policies to guide them. In some cases, I have modified policies to deal with particular situations. My humanistic side has permitted me to view employee's needs thoughtfully, ensuring a well-rounded view of their requests. My financial skills have sharpened as I have had to create and promote budgets, and scrutinize revenues and expenditures under the watchful public eye. Negotiating pricing for goods and services and offering bidding opportunities has honed my frugality with other people's money. Ascertaining unconventional funding sources has helped recover dwindling revenues. My never ending interaction with people has trained me to be diplomatic, caring, and improved my hearing, not just listening. I have advanced my political skills by dealing directly with upper level legislators and policy makers when defending local home rule, or putting forth proposed bills for the benefit of my community. Most importantly, I have learned what it means to provide services to the public in multiple and various ways.

Although my tenure might suggest that I may be an expert in my line of work, I will be the first to admit that my knowledge is fractional against others. I will continue to absorb information as time passes. Each day brings new situations that are challenging the limits of municipal services. I will continue to find ways to help people with their needs, by relying on other manager's ideas, and trying alternative concepts that have not been tried. In this profession, the learning will continue to evolve, and never end.

References

Maine Municipal Association. 2013. *The LPC handbook: MMA's Legislative Policy Committee.* Retrieved from Maine Municipal Association: http://memun.org/LegislativeAdvocacy/TheLPCHandbook.aspx

Haag, J. 1993. *The manager plan in Maine.* University of Maine.

ICMA. 2012, May 29. *Cost savings of intergovernmental contracts.* Retrieved from ICMA.com: http://icma.org/en/Article/102155/Cost_Savings_of_Intergovernmental_Contracts

Luthra, V. 2013. *Management by objectives definition.* Retrieved from Business Dictionary.com: http://www.businessdictionary.com/definition/management-byobjectives-MBO.html

Michael's Artifacts and Documents

Document 1	Employment Contract, 2001
Document 2	Employment Contract, 2008–11
Document 3	Employment Contract, 2011–14
Document 4	Shared Services Contract—Emergency Medical Services
Document 5	Shared Services Contract—Public Works
Document 6	Committee participation—School Law Training 2007, School Consolidation 2007, Regional Planning Committee 2008
Document 7	Committee participation—MMA Legislative Policy Committee

Document 8   Committee participation—Androscoggin Valley Council of Governments

Document 9   Committee participation—A.O.C. Rail Coalition

Document 10   Certification of Sworn Appointment, Treasurer

Document 11   Training Certification—Government Accounting 1 & 2

Document 12   Training Certification—Tax Law, 2005–2008

Document 13   Comprehensive Plan Approval – State Letter

Document 14   Public Meeting Minutes—Fireworks

Document 15   Reference Letter

Document 16   Certified Municipal Manager Certificate

Michael's Portfolio Assessment

Rubric Score: 28 out of 28

RUBRIC SCORES

Course Outcomes Identified and Addressed	4/4
Learning from Experience	4/4
Understanding of Theory and Practice	4/4
Reflection	4/4
Learning Application	4/4
Communication	4/4
Supporting Documentation	4/4

ASSESSOR WRITTEN FEEDBACK

The student demonstrates in a satisfactory way the core competencies required for PAD-332. He clearly outlines the course objectives and responds to them with clear, articulate explanations of his experience and understanding. The examples of his interactions and activities as Town Manager clearly fit the expectations for this course as he justifies his understanding of the types of governments, the relationship between government functions/offices, and the importance of citizen participation. In addition, his supportive documentation was appropriate and supportive to his portfolio.

Michael earned full credit for his portfolio.

6 APPLYING PORTFOLIO ASSESSMENT PRINCIPLES

This chapter provides an opportunity for you to put yourself in the expert assessor's shoes! A rubric is provided at the end of this chapter. Space is allowed for your notes.

Generally, assessors tell us it takes about two hours to evaluate a portfolio. Keep in mind that the assessors are faculty subject matter experts and have likely taught the course for which credit is being sought.

Student Portfolio Example #6—Lynn

Seeking Credit for: MGMT 3143 Human Resource Management

Course Description

Functions and problems involved in personnel management with emphasis placed upon recruitment, selection, management development, utilization of and accommodation to human resources by organizations. Prerequisite, MGMT 3153.

Learning Objectives

1. To provide a theoretical and practical understanding of HR management in both public and private sector organizations. (Business Knowledge)

2. To provide information on recruitment, selection, management development, and utilization of HR by organizations. (Business Knowledge, Critical Thinking)

3. To provide a framework in HR management that will serve as preparation for students interested in pursuing advanced courses in the HR field. (Critical Thinking)

4. To assist each student in developing an integrated personal philosophy of HR management by encouraging the study and integration of various ideas and concepts from different areas of the management literature. (Business Knowledge, Ethics)

Learning Narrative

Human Resource Management, 3143

The student's introduction works well to set the stage for the learning narrative, particularly in *giving the assessor a clear understanding of where her experiential learning has taken place.*

As a matter of a short introduction, my name is Lynn and I am currently seeking to complete a degree in interdisciplinary studies. I began college many years ago as a Health Services Administration major, but wound up working full time in a job where I never envisioned myself, that of a full-time police officer. I do possess an Associate of Applied Science in Criminal Justice degree (see Document 1), and I am now seeking to finally complete a bachelor degree in order to better present myself as a more viable candidate for additional promotion or other career endeavors.

I currently hold the rank of captain in my department, which is a medium sized police agency of one hundred and fifty-five officers and twenty-seven civilian support personnel. I have been part of the command staff for eight years and previously commanded the Professional Standards and Patrol divisions. I have over twenty-five years of service with the agency, and I have worked in a variety of supervisory and management positions. I have also served on the board of directors for various community organizations, such as CASA (Court Appointed Special Advocates) and the NEA Council on Family Violence, but my most recent service was two terms (four years) on the board of directors for the local United Way (see Document 2).

While my employment experience in management has all been with the same organization, the same basic principles would apply as would with any organization. There are so many elements that fall under the umbrella of human resources, it will be difficult to cover them in such a short space, but in the following pages, I will discuss my knowledge of the material contained in the course **MGMT 3143—Human Resource Management**.

The student references different **theories and relates them back to her experience**. This shows transference of learning and her ability to reflect upon the theories.

The text for this course begins by examining some of the challenges facing companies today as they try to develop and implement or upgrade and maintain human resource strategies and tactics that maintain customer driven perspectives. While the pioneers of scientific management like Fredrick Taylor began the discipline seeking for increased efficiency and productivity, current human resource management practices are based on the human relations school of work by pioneers like Elton Mayo and Mary Follett.

These practices focus on not only the concern for human feelings, attitudes, and relationships but also in obtaining and retaining skilled workers. When considering the HR strategy that would best describe my own agency, one has to consider that we are actually one unit of an overall public entity that is entrusted with the care of daily service to the citizens of the city. Of the three business unit strategies formulated by Porter, Milles, & Snow, my agency would follow the Overall Cost Leadership model (Gomez-Mejia, Balkin, and Cardy 2013). While we may occasionally employ tactics that would be common to a Differentiation or Focus strategy in order to attract businesses, our treatment of our employees and daily operations, must be focused on getting the most bang for the taxpayer buck, since our operations are under constant public scrutiny for cost effectiveness.

While much of my exposure to daily human resource matters is related to the public sector employment, many aspects remain the same as they would for a private business. The course description for this class includes all the fundamentals of human resource including recruiting, staffing, employee development, compensation, employee performance, and managing discipline. Most all of the material covered is among the topics and training that have been provided to me through my employer, specifically delivered through the city's knowledgeable human resource department. The current and previous human resource managers for the city that I work for all came from the private sector and utilized many of the same materials and documentation and shared their expertise as they worked with managers and supervisors on various matters. The current human resource technician was gracious enough to provide me with a letter of recommendation, asserting my knowledge of this material (see Document 3).

While some of the benefits for police officers such as retirement, vacation, and sick time are regulated by state law, the compensation and benefits for civilian employees within the department are regulated in much the same way as they would be in private sector businesses. The Fair Labor Standards Act (FLSA) and Equal Pay Act (EPA) set the minimums and private businesses and governments are left to utilize what resources they can to compete for and retain desirable employees. Workers compensation, USERRA, and other issues are also issues that are regulated by law and as such remain somewhat standard from private sector to public employment. The city human resources office oversees a program of continuing education training required by city management for supervisors, which allows the city to achieve uniform HR service and management with few actual HR dedicated employees. Upper level supervisors for various city departments are required to attend various training and re-training on a number of issues from workplace safety to new human resource related regulations and laws in general. Some of the training is readily available from outside sources, but some is also done by the human resource department itself. At least one of the courses I attended that included a significant amount of human resource management related material was a 60-hour certificate series offered by our local university that had both public and private sector attendees (Course Objectives 1 & 3) (see Documents, 4, 5, 6, 7, 8 & 9).

Managing resources and guiding employees through certain HR related tasks, such as completing benefits paperwork and conducting workman's comp and safety violation investigations, helped me more thoroughly understand the role of human resources management. Many more HR related issues were revealed after I was again promoted and then became involved in recruiting, hiring, and discipline issues with the staff. The area of recruiting, selection, and hiring is one that I enjoy and recognize as invaluable to creating a strong foundation for the agency. While maintaining fair employment practices is a must, my own profession involves a situation where Bona Fide Occupational Qualifications (BFOQ) come into play because of certain state laws concerning citizenship and physical expectations for an officer, but there are still a certain number of positions that do not contain those restrictions. As a public sector employer, we also try to remain mindful of the importance of recruiting from several available workforce pools. Even before seeking accreditation for our agency, we already publicly affirmed our commitment to being an equal opportunity employer and made certain that staff members, such as myself, who are actively involved in recruiting and hiring employees attend training and are familiar with EEOC and other HR law related to hiring (see Document 10).

When I found myself in charge of recruiting and selection several years ago, I could see that one area where we encountered challenges was in maintaining racial and ethnic diversity. The problem was not in that we turned minority applicants away, our problem was that we received very few applications from minorities. I began by contacting community leaders, as well as minority groups at the local university and encouraged their input as well as their support. We began to become more heavily involved in community job fairs and actually began a practice of contacting potential applicants who had not necessarily expressed an interest in law enforcement previously. As the stakeholders we sought to form relationships with became more familiar with our desire to seek out minority applicants, we began to see a slight rise in the number of minority applicants, a trend that has continued and we now feel that the community recognizes our willingness to hire minorities and are comfortable seeking out employment here. Our most recent testing cycle reflects that increased confidence, as we had a record number of minority applicants (Course Objective 2) (see Document 11, Recruitment Plan 2007—Document 12, Testing Cycle Report 2011).

Experienced and well educated applicants are always welcomed by any business, but regardless of whether or not the applicants that come to us are experienced, we always want to do our best to ensure that they are a good fit to the profession, since we will have approximately nine months involved in training before they are actually a working officer. The focus has to be on not only selecting those candidates that possess the skill set to be good candidates, but on training them to use and hone those skills that will make them successful employees. While much of our focus is on the officers, since their training is so costly, we also utilize many of the same recruiting and training strategies for civilian employees. Careful planning and maintenance of continuity in training then follows that will help us achieve successful employees (see Document 13, Local Newspaper Article).

In an era when companies find themselves competing for the best employees, companies have embarked on offering alternative, perhaps non-financial, incentives that give employees more of a feeling of ownership and being a part of a family. Perks such as onsite daycare and automotive service may not be feasible for all businesses, but with a little ingenuity, many can offer benefits to employees that will impart some of the same feelings of value. As personal examples, my employer offers incentives such as allowing non-probationary employees the option of taking their work vehicle home and dry cleaning of their work uniforms. The law enforcement profession is recognized as being one where daily stress can quickly become a crippling disability. In the book *Emotional Survival*, Dr. Kevin Gilmartin (2012) referred to this as "the hypervigilance biological rollercoaster." Fortunately, my employer is one that has established a successful Employee Assistance Program (EAP), and we are also able to provide our employees with access to the program at no or very little cost. City training was provided, and I passed along this training by completing interdepartmental training for lower level supervisors. Additionally, in order to take advantage of this program from an organizational standpoint, I formulated an interdepartmental employee early warning system so that issues that might arise while an officer was deployed with various shifts or units would not get lost as they switched assignments. If such issues are identified, employees can be referred to the EAP (see Documents 14, 15 & 16, EAP Training Documents, EAP Referral, & EWS Policy).

While hiring employees begins the foundation, and training is designed to ensure competent and knowledgeable employees, determining how to utilize or deploy those employees is an integral part of maintaining a cost efficient business and central to actually gaining the most benefit from the human resources available. A work flow analysis should be conducted frequently in order to maintain a desired level of productivity. Business demands change and those changes have to be accommodated, which could be achieved through a number of methods, including a reengineering of certain business processes, adjusting schedules or seeking out new technologies that increase unit efficiency. I have twice had the opportunity to take a role in workload analysis studies conducted by private contractors hired by the city. As the department liaison to the city employee representative committee at the time, during one of those studies, I was heavily involved and got to experience firsthand the meetings and strategy sessions as the purpose for the study was developed and outlined, a contractor was selected and the analysis itself was conducted as part of an overall action plan to implement an upgraded city wide pay scale. However, there can also be a much more usable and perhaps beneficial product created when you invest in conducting your own study as well. Since you have the ability to study the issues pertinent to your organization and have a more thorough understanding of the nature of the work, such an analysis can not only be enlightening, but is useful for achieving maximum productivity. Part of my assigned tasks as an administrative supervisor for the Chief was to conduct an internal workload analysis and produce a report outlining the current situation and formulate recommendations that reflected what my department hoped to be able to accomplish by reformulating their deployment strategy (see Document 17, Manpower & Deployment Report).

High performance corporations are normally filled with highly motivated and highly productive employees. While businesses should be concerned with maintaining policy compliance and productivity, they also have to maintain positive employee relations. Training people in the proper methods of completing the various aspects of their job provides a foundation that should be built on continually. Effective communication of policies, rules, and expectations have to take place in a timely and consistent manner in order to ensure everyone has an understanding or what it takes to maintain compliance and successfully do their job. However, because retention of skilled employees is so important, it becomes mandatory that companies and organizations continue to seek alternative ways to increase employee job satisfaction. Large salaries and heaping benefits packages won't be enough to retain an employee if their job satisfaction falls below what they deem to be an acceptable level. Positive motivation becomes key to producing employees who are satisfied with their job.

Maintaining a positive work environment and keeping up employee job satisfaction is not only a matter of a large salary or a comfortable chair. Some companies turn to working retreats in order to bring work into a more positive atmosphere. Still others sponsor a variety of company activities, perhaps contests or picnics, that foster a sense of belonging and unity among employees. In some environments, lack of group cohesion can result in creating an environment that is not only detrimental to job satisfaction, it is detrimental to productivity. When a small group of employees were reassigned to my supervision a number of years ago, they were at a stage where the productivity of the group was not even at an acceptable minimum. Years of dissension and bickering about job responsibilities had eroded group unity to the point of almost nonexistence. I afforded them the opportunity of closing their office for one hour a week, as long as all were willing to spend that time together as a group, to eat lunch, go to an event, or perhaps volunteer. In less than three months, it was no longer necessary to encourage them to get together as a group because they began to plan outings and projects on their own. While there may not have been a significant increase in productivity, complaints decreased and the negative stigma of their unit disappeared (see Document 18, Photo).

Paid volunteerism, such as what I encouraged in my problem group, is an emerging trend companies are turning to in order to fulfill ethical obligations in their communities. Allowing employees to volunteer for various non-profit organizations and events is yet another method to boost employee morale and self-esteem, since there can be tremendous emotional benefit as the employee is allowed to give back without having to take time off. The loss of the employee for these short periods of time are likely no more financially taxing than the average vacation or sick leave, and it places a positive light on the company as the employees and the community have the opportunity to see employers as generous and caring. As a board member for the United Way, I am aware of first hand, how we relied on paid volunteers or what we refer to as loaned executives. On page 333 and 334, the text for this course relates a number of success stories where companies participated in paid volunteerism and mentions that "...companies believe they're getting something back...employees with enhanced leadership skills and broadened global outlooks" (Gomez-Mejia, et al. 2013).

Part of ensuring the success of current work practices is in deciding on a fair and reasonable method of measuring employee productivity and performance. Rating scales, such as rank ordering, paired comparison, the forced choice method, Forced Distribution, (Cordner and Scarborough 2010) or Trait appraisal (Gomez-Mejia, et al. 2013.) Fyfe, et al. 1997.) are among the methods that have been devised for measuring employee performance. All of these methods and others are among those outlined in a number of texts I have had to study for promotional testing over the years, and at different times, my organization has utilized a few different types. The biggest issue with any type of rating or evaluation system is in maintaining the continuity among different raters. Currently, my agency actually utilizes a combination of evaluation techniques depending on the complexity of the job assignment. While everyone receives at least an annual evaluation that is a forced choice type measurement, probationary employees may be subjected to quarterly, weekly, or daily evaluations during different training cycles. Additionally, officers responding to the varied situations encountered during daily patrol are required to participate in a minimum number of activities in order to maintain certain productivity levels. The types of activities they participate in afford a great deal of officer choice and, outside of responding to specific calls from citizens, are optional.

Recognition awards are not only a means of rewarding above average performance, they also provide a key way of increasing positive employee relations. Such awards do not necessarily have to be accompanied by a financial award and can be seen as a means of carrying out the old adage "punish in private, praise in public." Systems that relate pay to job performance could actually increase job stress and lower job satisfaction because the production of a work unit becomes the focus, often times at the expense of other employees or even the customers. Pay based rewards such as bonuses or profit sharing are not something that can be offered by a government entity such as the one where I work, but merit based pay is one method of encouraging increased performance through increased pay. Again, challenges persist as we work through how best to measure employee performance and establish certain benchmarks for determining awards in any such merit system. In my own customer service oriented type of profession, balancing between workers who are thorough in completing a task as opposed to those who haste to move on to the next assignment in order to increase raw statistics, can result in a less than favorable completion of assigned tasks, even though productivity numbers may look favorable.

Unfortunately, sometimes no amount of monitoring and motivation can keep some employees from failing to avoid disciplinary action. While normally only a very small part of human resource management, employee discipline can be a source of civil action if handled incorrectly. However, it can also be an additional source of job dissatisfaction if other employees perceive that such actions are handled incorrectly or unfairly. While not among my favorite tasks, I have been involved in a number of employee disciplinary proceedings from informal performance reviews, misconduct investigations, as well as some terminations and unemployment hearings (see Document 19). Proper documentation is key when employee discipline actions are required not only for the case at hand, but also to guard against possible allegations of negligent hiring and retention.

Over the years, I have gained both knowledge and experience in management. From working in my own public sector service profession, to dealing with volunteers in small and large scale events and organizations, to some early experience with a private sector employer. The control and compliance culture of the Theory X generation that permeated my work experience as a young person is slowly giving way to what I perceive as a more palatable and efficient structure of coordination and control. As I encounter more candidates and employees from the younger Y generation, it is obvious that my own style of being less controlling and focusing more on motivation and increasing job satisfaction is working to my benefit (Objective 4). Effectiveness and productivity can be hindered if creativity and performance are choked out. Gaining the most from the human resource of an organization can only be achieved when you acknowledge the value of individual employees and create an environment where they are nurtured to embrace a feeling of personal accomplishment as they work to further the goals of the organization.

Bibliography

Cordner, G., and Scarborough, K. 2010. *Police administration*. Cincinnati, OH: Anderson.

Fyfe, J., Greene, J., Walsh, W., Wilson, O., and McLaren, R. 1997. *Police administration*. Boston, MA: McGraw-Hill.

Gilmartin, K. 2012. *Emotional survival for law enforcement*. Tucson, AZ: E-S Press.

Gomez-Mejia, L., Balkin, D., and Cardy, R. 2013. *Managing human resources*. Boston, MA: Pearson.

Your Assessment

Now that you have read Lynn's learning narrative, it is important for you to review the documentation provided and use the rubric to score the portfolio. **Here is a list of documentation items provided:**

1. Criminal Justice Associate of Applied Science Degree
2. United Way Board of Directors Photo (including the student)
3. Recommendation Letter from City HR Tech (below)
4. Management and Leadership Series course certificate
5. Course completion certificate for HR continuing education class (60 contact hours)
6. E-mail in reference to in-house HR training attended by the student
7. E-mail in reference to in-house USERRA training
8. Certificate from safety training (OSHA)
9. Outline for another in-house employee safety training
10. Certificate for Employment Background Investigation training
11. Recruitment Plan written by the student
12. Testing and Recruiting Plan written by the student
13. Article in local newspaper about recruitment, including a section where the student is quoted
14. E-mail in reference to EAP (Employee Assistance Program) training attended by the student
15. Example of where student used the training when making a referral to EAP
16. Policy, written by the student, for the department concerning the "Employee Early Warning System" that includes when to make a referral to EAP
17. Manpower and Deployment Report written by the student
18. Photo of ladies who were part of a dysfunctional unit that the student worked with and brought together as not only a functional unit, but they even continued to interact outside of work
19. E-mail regarding disciplinary action to be completed
20. Letter of Verification (see next page)

On City Letterhead

August 19, 2014

To Whom It May Concern:

As Human Resources/Safety Technician for the City for over eight years, I have worked with a number of supervisors concerning various aspects of human resource management. I personally have over 15 years of experience in human resource management in both the public and private sectors and have practiced and taught many aspects of such in a variety of situations. I have worked with Captain [student's name] in a number of situations and I have knowledge of capabilities or have personally seen her practice a variety of human resource functions.

It is my understanding that she has requested that I provide a statement of my knowledge of this individual's abilities because she is seeking college credit for her experience and understanding of the concepts of management of human resources related functions. She has provided me with a copy of her portfolio materials and allowed me to review the text for the course, and I am confident that her understanding of the subject material for this course matches the requirements.

Respectfully.

Signature Here

HR/Safety Technician

Recognizing that you are likely not an expert in the management of human resources and you probably haven't taught the course, it is still a good exercise to assess a portfolio based upon a rubric. This rubric is very simple (and if you were doing this in real life, the rubric would likely be more sophisticated).

Practice Rubric

Criteria	4 Exceptional Performance	3 Above Average Performance	2 Addressed, but Room for Improvement	0 Not addressed or Not acceptable
Course Objectives, Learning Outcomes, or Competencies Identified and Addressed				
Learning from Experience				
Understanding Theory and Practice				
Reflection Is Evident				
Learning Application				
College-Level Writing and Communication				
Supporting Documentation				

Total Score _____ (maximum score is 28)

Credit Recommendation

☐ Credit Recommended

☐ Credit Denied

Written Feedback for Student

_____

_____

_____

_____

_____

To see actual completed assessment, go to Appendix C.

CHAPTER 7

FREQUENTLY ASKED QUESTIONS

At first blush, it is easy to misunderstand portfolio assessment. Throughout this book you can find answers to almost any question regarding portfolio assessment. Here are a few frequently asked questions for your consideration.

1. **Is it possible for students who are seeking credit for skills-based courses to use portfolio assessment?**

   Yes, it is possible. In fact, in some instances (fine arts, for example) a portfolio may be the best way to showcase college-level skills. For courses such as welding, students can upload videos of themselves preparing to weld, demonstrating different types of welds, and then demonstrating the strength of the weld.

   Please see Appendix D for an example of a successful technical or CTE (Career and Technical Education) course portfolio.

2. **How can a portfolio assessment be objective?**

   Portfolios, as the examples in this book demonstrate, directly link to the syllabus' learning outcomes, objectives, or competencies. When the learning outcomes are clearly stated, a student is better able to directly address them. Using a rubric for the assessment removes much of the subjectivity. It is important to note that the student's portfolio is usually not graded; it is a credit or no credit decision. The student's work must be equivalent or comparable to a student who passes the course ("C" grade or better) when taken in the traditional format. There are weaknesses inherent in every form of assessment. However, the learning portfolio is comparable to a final, comprehensive term paper, something that is not always required for courses, particularly at the lower level.

   > "The assessment of a portfolio can't just be a seat-of-your-pants, gut feeling kind of thing. Not only does an assessor need to determine whether a student knows as much as he or she would have learned in the equivalent course, the assessor needs to be able to document that student's mastery of the relevant learning outcomes. The process of evaluating a portfolio is important, and it's not something you can do just because you know your subject. It requires another set of skills on top of that, and an understanding of how prior learning assessment works."
   >
   > **Marc P. Singer**
   > Vice Provost, Center for the Assessment of Learning
   > Thomas Edison State University

3. **How can portfolio assessment be a legitimate academic process?**

   Portfolio assessment (as noted in Chapter 1) grew out of a major research project of ETS and the College Board to determine whether learning attained outside of the college environment could be assessed with academic rigor for college credit. The project's base line established that it could be done, and *done well.* Today, thousands of students have benefitted from earning credit through portfolio assessment and gone on to earn their degrees. Faculty assessors have assessed portfolios and found them to be, for the most part, very impressive.

4. Is portfolio assessment easier than taking and passing the course?

Portfolio students and assessors alike will tell you that developing a portfolio is not the easy way to credit. In fact, some students decide that they would rather take the course because writing a portfolio is too time consuming and difficult. A portfolio requires the student to address every learning outcome with compelling concise writing and documentation. There is no mid-term or formative assessment to help the student stay on track. The discipline, organizational, and writing skills required for a portfolio are often skills that not only demonstrate college-level work but generally are equivalent to upper division work.

5. How can a complete stranger assess a student the way I do for my course?

When a well-designed rubric is used with thoughtful consideration, a qualified assessor can come very close to arriving at the same assessment as you do, particularly if your syllabus has well-articulated specific learning outcomes described.

6. How can portfolio students do as well as students in a traditional classroom when they don't have the benefit of class discussions and interactions with an instructor?

There can be something lost for students who are not exposed to classroom lectures and discussions, **but the *process or inputs* of learning should not matter. What a student learns, the actual learning outcomes and competencies, is more important than how or where the student learned it.** Demonstrating the outcomes at a "C" grade level or above is what is required to earn college credit.

As one of our portfolio assessment students is fond of asking those who question portfolio assessment, "Can you write a 15-page narrative about each course you took in college, and can you provide evidence of that knowledge?" His point is clear: the portfolio assessment process is rigorous and requires evidence of learning in the form of artifacts, or proof, that students can demonstrate what they know.

Marie A. Cini, PhD

Provost and Senior Vice President for Academic Affairs

University of Maryland University College

7. How can I explain portfolio assessment to my colleagues and to students?

Portfolio assessment is for students who have significant learning and experience in a subject area that aligns with a specific course, courses, or curriculum, such as competency-based education. Students must describe their learning gained from experience, such as on the job, and demonstrate their learning is equivalent and comparable to the learning demonstrated by students who take the course or are awarded credit for competencies. The student must essentially lay out his or her case for credit learning outcome by learning outcome and provide evidence to support his or her claim. The portfolio is complete when the student has written about his or her learning at the college level in a thoughtful way aligned directly to the course outcomes, objectives, or competencies. An assessor, who is a faculty subject matter expert, makes an evaluation to determine if credit can be awarded. Portfolios are assessed using a rubric. Portfolio assessment is not as concerned with the inputs (like seat time) as it is with the learning outcomes.

8. Do assessors ever award partial credit, such as 2 credits for a 3-credit hour course?

It is generally an *all credit or no credit* proposition. Earning credit for part of a course will not help the student (unless it's an elective) since the student needs credit for the whole course. When the rubric is sound, partial credit is not possible.

9. How are portfolio credits represented on the transcript?

Transcription processes vary from college to college, but generally speaking, portfolio credits appear on the transcript with some sort of a prior learning assessment designation. Since the portfolio is awarded credit, it is likely to appear as a P for "pass" on the transcript. The name of the course and course number appear on the transcript. Block credit is not advised because registrars need to assure that credit is not duplicated.

10. **How much do faculty assessors get paid to assess a portfolio?**

In a recent research brief by CAEL, institutional leaders were asked this very question. Compensation for portfolio assessment varies from a range of no dollars (considered as part of a faculty member's contract or regular work responsibilities) to $250 per portfolio (Klein-Collins 2015).

What is the typical profile of a student who is likely to be successful going the portfolio assessment route?

Portfolio Assessment Student Profile

- Adult learner with significant work experience
- May be a military service member or veteran
- Likely has career experience with increasing responsibility over the course of five years or more
- A person who is not afraid of writing at the college level or has successfully completed English Composition
- A person who has taken some college courses before
- A self-motivated learner who is interested in accelerating degree completion
- A student who has taken a portfolio assessment course or workshop

11. **What happens to the portfolios once they have been assessed?**

Copies of portfolios or digital portfolios should be archived by the college or university according to their records retention policy. It is important to have the portfolios available should an accrediting team happen to pull the student record of a portfolio student in its regular accrediting visit. Students, on the other hand, often use their portfolios to show employers, prospective employers, and/or educators.

8 TAKING PORTFOLIO ASSESSMENT INTO THE FUTURE

The future of portfolio assessment is likely to be one of continuous innovation, refinement and new applications. Up until the last five years or so, portfolio assessment was a process that was virtually unchanged since its pilot at ETS in 1974 (see Appendix A). The reason for its lack of modification is that it has had to be linked so directly to traditional academic practices. Now, with hundreds of new academic innovations in front of us, new technology, and new voices in the academy, portfolio assessment is ripe for innovation.

Technology has enabled many advancements in portfolio assessment in the past decade. Portfolios used to be comprised of notebooks containing a student's learning narrative (maybe even typed on a typewriter) and documentation. The notebook had to be literally passed along from the PLA director to the faculty assessor and back again. The student would be notified when the assessment was complete. All aspects of the portfolio were "manual" including submitting the credit approval through the Registrar's Office for posting the credit to the transcript. If the portfolio got "stuck" along the way, such as being left in a faculty mailbox for days, tracking down the portfolio would be a time-consuming challenge. Portfolios were often copied to be filed according to records retention policies. The students received their originals back along with the assessment.

The use of digital portfolios is gaining traction at today's colleges and universities. Digital portfolios enable tracking at every step of the way. Much of the communication is done via e-mail (including automated messages) and the portfolio can be digitally archived. Portfolios are electronically routed to the various personnel who serve as the checks and balances for the process as well as being routed to the appropriate faculty assessor. The now digital narrative can be submitted to plagiarism detection services online.

Another important benefit of today's technology for portfolio assessment is the ease with which data can be collected. Here are some various reports that can be pulled using today's technologies:

- Credit Awarded/No Credit rates
- Most popular courses for portfolio assessment
- Portfolio student demographics
- Credits awarded per discipline or academic department/division
- When portfolios are most often developed—such as in the spring or fall, first year or senior year, first 30 credit hours or last 30 credit hours, etc.
- Academic outcomes of portfolio assessment students, such as retention rates, number of courses taken after the portfolio, GPAs, success in future courses, and degree/credential completion rates

Technology has enabled the portfolio development and assessment process to be a more easily administered system. It also tends to be more student friendly, in that the technology prompts students throughout their experience to remember documentation; address every objective, outcome, or competency; and to meet any deadlines. The same is true for the faculty assessor experience. The technology enables the faculty assessor to do the assessment any time, anywhere.

"I believe that portfolio assessment (PA) will become increasingly important in a competency-based educational future. PA very much aligns with the idea that learning is more than simply recalling facts; true learning requires contextualizing action within theory demonstrating the ability to apply knowledge to new settings. PA requires that level of reflection and insight. In many ways PA is a process whose time has come."

Marie A. Cini, PhD

Provost and Senior Vice President for Academic Affairs

University of Maryland University College

One of the most important innovations in postsecondary education today is competency-based education (CBE), which could be viewed as portfolio assessment's younger sibling. CBE enables students to demonstrate their learning in different ways to move through their curriculum based upon competency attainment. Students who have already mastered a competency can demonstrate it, be assessed, and move on to more challenging competencies. The competency demonstrations may take the form of an assignment, such as a case study, or an assessment, or maybe even a narrative similar to what we might see in a portfolio. These demonstrations open up new possibilities for portfolio assessment that may be less writing intensive.

One such demonstration is the structured interview. Comprised of thoughtful questions developed by faculty subject matter experts, a student can be interviewed by the assessor and respond to the questions verbally, without having to write an extensive learning narrative. These assessments can be done face-to-face on Skype or in-person. Questions are derived from the learning outcomes and should be made available to the student in advance of the assessment (as well as the rubric for scoring the assessment). Individualized assessments for technical skills, such as advanced manufacturing courses, allow for a student to be assessed in a lab with faculty observers.

One aspect of portfolio assessment that causes some consternation with students is its "all or nothing" approach to credit. Competency-based assessment allows the student to demonstrate the competencies required for a course and earn acknowledgement for the completion of those competencies. A competency-based portfolio can do the same thing. Rather than award partial credit to a student who clearly demonstrates college-level learning but is missing the mark by one or two competencies, a student can simply complete the remaining competencies once he or she has had a chance to learn the material. Once learned, the student can be re-assessed to earn full credit.

Other technology-based innovations include enabling students to upload videos as part of the documentation or artifacts required for the portfolio. The videos range from public speaking videos to the demonstration of particular college-level skills to technical videos that are based upon the student using a particular piece of equipment or specialized software.

Portfolio Assessment as Part of a Larger Framework

Considerable work is underway to align learning from various sources into frameworks that clarify how courses and learning activities are viewed from a more strategic and unifying vantage point. The frameworks are hoped to ease questions of transferability among courses, as well as how one credential might compare to another credential. A particularly applicable framework for prior learning is the Global Learning Qualifications Framework (GLQF). For more infor-

mation on the GLQF, go to http://www.esc.edu/suny-real/global
-learning-qualifications-framework/. See also Figure 5.

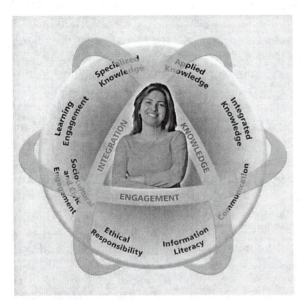

FIGURE 5. *The Global Learning Qualifications Framework*

A Vision for the Future

Imagine, if you will, an Assessment Center on every campus and available online. This center is open to all students. The center represents an institutional approach to recognizing prior learning and the importance of academically rigorous assessment. Students of all ages, backgrounds, and experiences may challenge competency sets tied to courses, course sequences, badges, microcredentials, certificates, and degrees. The center is the heart of the institution; essentially institutionalizing assessment for personal growth, development, and lifelong learning. Students may take nationally standardized exams, such as CLEP, DSST, or UExcels, or challenge exams for courses. They may choose to have a structured interview for a set of competencies or a course or prepare a portfolio with guidance from the Center.

Overall, the goal would be for every student to be on a personalized postsecondary pathway. The pathway takes into consideration student mobility, thus capturing credits into various credentials (from badges to degrees) along the way. It is conceivable that students will be more successful when they've been afforded the opportunity to have their prior or even new learning assessed and documented. One might extrapolate from the research that student retention and persistence rates will improve, as well as degree completion (Klein-Collins 2010).

Considering today's focus on improving both K-12 and postsecondary education, it is also conceivable that students as young as recent high school graduates will benefit from the services of the Assessment Center approach (well beyond today's use of placement tests). Imagine the benefits possible for workforce development. It's all possible, particularly with new technologies and a greater emphasis on prior learning assessment.

In Jamie Merisotis's book, *America Needs Talent: Attracting, Educating & Deploying the 21st Century Workforce* (2015), Mr. Merisotis includes prior learning assessment in the new paradigm for higher education. Whether portfolio assessment is a stand alone program or fully integrated in institutional culture, portfolio assessment is moving into mainstream higher education in ways that might not have been predicted even a decade ago. As an example, the University of Maryland University College (UMUC) is "moving to a model whereby we assume most adult students can benefit from portfolio assessment and will help a larger number of our students to include portfolio assessment as part their degree planning. The process that students go through as they develop their portfolios also increases their self-understanding and helps them clarify and sharpen their career goals," according to Marie Cini, Provost and Senior Vice President at UMUC. Dr. Cini goes on to say, "Providing portfolio assessment is critical to the success of our UMUC students. Our students are adults who have considerable knowledge accumulated outside of the traditional college classroom. By offering portfolio assessment to our students, they are able to demonstrate what they know for college credit. This respects the adult learner and helps them achieve a college degree in a more reasonable amount of time, given all that they are balancing in their lives."

Portfolio assessment, now and in the future, will continue to expand opportunities for students who are learning on the job, in volunteer roles, and through independent self-directed study to earn college credit toward degrees. As more and more colleges and universities embrace portfolio assessment, more and more students will achieve their educational goals of earning college degrees.

"Indeed, it's becoming increasingly clear that "college-level learning" does not even need to take place in a traditional institution of higher education as we know it. With the emergence of trends like taking a person's prior military, education, national service, or work experience and assigning actual credit or value to it in a college context – prior learning assessment – we see the emergence of a new paradigm. In this new world, providing students smarter pathways into and through higher education will be critical. All learning should count; ..."

Jamie Merisotis

President and CEO

The Lumina Foundation

America Needs Talent: Attracting, Educating & Deploying the 21st Century Workforce (2015, p. 72)

REFERENCES

Bamford-Rees, D. 2009. Timeline: Thirty-five years of prior learning assessment: 1973–2008. In D. M. Hart and J. H. H., *Prior learning portfolios: A representative collection* pp. 9–10. Chicago, IL: The Council for Adult and Experiential Learning & Kendall Hunt Professional.

Colvin, J. 2006. *Earn college credit for what you know.* Chicago, IL: CAEL.

Cordner, G., and Scarborough, K. 2010. *Police administration.* Cincinnati, OH: Anderson.

Fiddler, M., Marienau, C., and Whitaker, U. 2006. *Assessing learning: Standards, principles, & procedures* 2nd ed.. Dubuque, IA: Kendall/Hunt.

Fyfe, J., Greene, J., Walsh, W., Wilson, O., and McLaren, R. 1997. *Police administration.* Boston: McGraw-Hill.

Gilmartin, K. 2012. *Emotional survival for law enforcement.* Tucson, AZ: E-S Press.

Gomez-Mejia, L., Balkin, D., and Cardy, R. 2013. *Managing human resources.* Boston, MA: Pearson.

Hart, D. M., and Hickerson, J. H. 2009. *Prior learning portfolios: A representative collection.* Chicago, IL: CAEL.

Kasworm, C. E., and Marienau, C. M. 1997, Fall. Principles for assessment of adult learning. *New directions for adult and continuing education 199775,* 5–16.

Klein-Collins, R. 2010. *Fueling the race to postsecondary success: A 48-institution study of prior learning assessment and adult student outcomes.* Chicago, IL: CAEL.

Klein-Collins, R. 2015. *PLA is your business: Pricing and other considerations for the PLA business model – Findings from a national survey of PLA program leaders.* Chicago, IL: CAEL.

Merisotis, J. P. 2015. *America needs talent: Attracting, educating & deploying the 21st-century workforce.* New York, NY: RosettaBooks.

Schroeder, D., and Lombardo, F. 2006. *Management and supervision of L.E. personnel.* Charlottesville, VA: Gould.

Snyder, T. D., and Dillow, S.A. 2015. *Digest of education statistics 2013* NCES 2015-011. National Center for Education Statistics, Institute of Education Sciences, US Department of Education. Washington, DC. Retrieved from http://nces.ed.gov/fastfacts/display.asp?id=98

Tennessee Higher Education Commission. 2015, September 7. *Funding formula analysis: Outcomes-based formula narrative.* Retrieved from http://tn.gov/assets/entities/thec/attachments/1-Outcomes_Based_Formula_Narrative_-_for_website.pdf

Williams, C. 2013. *MGMT 5: Principles of management.* Mason, OH: Cengage Learning.

Williams, J. P. 2014, September 22. College of tomorrow: The changing demographics of the student body. *US News and World Report.* Retrieved September 4, 2015, from http://www.usnews.com/news/college-of-tomorrow/articles/2014/09/22/college-of-tomorrow-the-changing-demographics-of-the-student-body

Appendix A—PLA
Historical Timeline

1940s[12]

1944   Servicemen's Readjustment Act or GI Bill

1945   American Council on Education (ACE) begins evaluating military training for college credit recommendations

1946   One million GIs are using GI Bill benefits to attend college

1950s

1950   Two million GIs are using GI Bill benefits to attend college

1955   Advanced Placement (AP) Exams

1960s

Explosion of community colleges

1963   New York Board of Regents found CPEP – College Proficiency Examination Program (General Education Exams)

1964   Higher Education Act expands access to postsecondary education

1967   College Level Proficiency Exams (CLEP) become available

1968   Excelsior College Nursing Examinations become available

1970s

Empire State College, Thomas Edison State College, Charter Oak State College, Metropolitan State College, and Regents External Degree Program are founded to provide alternative pathways for adults to earn degrees. What is now called the National College Credit Recommendation Service was also founded.

1972   First degrees conferred by the Regents College

1973   Commission on Non-Traditional Study
        Office of External Degree Programs (ETS)

1974   ETS launch of the CAEL Project

1977   CAEL becomes its own entity with Morris Keaton as its executive director

1978   Kellogg-funded Institutional Development Program (IDP) launched by CAEL

1979   AACRAO, ACE, and CHEA endorse PLA and CAEL's Quality Principles

---

[12] The information in this timeline is from "Timeline: Thirty-five years of prior learning assessment: 1973 to 2008 by Diana Bamford-Rees, in *Prior learning portfolios: A representative collection* by Denise M. Hart and Jerry H. Hickerson 2009 p. 9-10, published by CAEL and Kendall Hunt.

1980s

Numerous publications and PLA surveys conducted by CAEL

1985	First edition of *Earn College Credit for What You Know* is published by CAEL
1989	First edition of *Assessing Learning: Standards, Principles & Procedures* is published by CAEL

1990s

1990	Tim Berners Lee invents the term *World Wide Web* and the first website is launched
	Pamela Tate becomes president of CAEL
1994	Online courses emerge
1995	Western Governors University is launched

2000s

2000	CAEL launches online PLA certificate program with DePaul University
2009	President Obama issues the College Completion Challenge to increase degree/credential attainment in the United States to 60 percent by 2025
2010	Landmark PLA study is published: *Fueling the Race to Postsecondary Success*
2011	Founding of LearningCounts.org
	First MOOCs emerge
	States begin looking at systematic approach to PLA (Wisconsin, Tennessee, Colorado, Ohio, Minnesota, Maine, Montana, Oregon, Washington, etc.)
2012	First direct assessment competency-based education program is approved by the Department of Education
2013	CAEL launches Competency-Based Education Quick Start professional development programs for 21 colleges, universities, and systems

Appendix B—CAEL's 10 Standards for Assessing Learning[13]

1. Credit or competencies are awarded only for evidence of learning, not for experience or time spent.

2. Assessment is integral to learning because it leads to and enables future learning.

3. Assessment is based on criteria for outcomes that are clearly articulated and shared among constituencies.

4. The determination of credit awards and competence levels must be made by appropriate subject matter and academic and credentialing experts.

5. Assessment advances the broader purpose of equity and access for diverse individuals and groups.

6. Institutions proactively provide guidance and support for learners' full engagement in the assessment process.

7. Assessment policies and procedures are the result of inclusive deliberation and are shared with all constituencies.

8. Fees charged for assessment should be based on the services performed in the process and not determined by the amount of credit awarded.

9. All practitioners involved in the assessment process pursue and receive adequate training and continuing professional development for the functions they perform.

10. Assessment programs should be regularly monitored, reviewed, evaluated, and revised to respond to institutional and learner needs.

---

[13] The Standards are from *Assessing Learning: Quality Standards and Institutional Commitment* (3d Ed.). Younger, D. & Marienau, C. (2017)

Appendix C—
Assessment Example

Actual Assessment of Lynn's Portfolio for MGMT 3143 Human Resource Management

Lynn's Portfolio Assessment (MGMT 3143 Human Resource Management)

Rubric Score: 25 out of 28

RUBRIC SCORES

Course Outcomes Identified and Addressed	4/4
Learning from Experience	3/4
Understanding of Theory and Practice	4/4
Reflection	3/4
Learning Application	4/4
Communication	3/4
Supporting Documentation	4/4

ASSESSOR WRITTEN FEEDBACK

This student presented a very professional portfolio that demonstrated her knowledge of human resource theory and practical application of theory to law enforcement, specifically a city police unit. Well done!

Lynn earned 3 credit hours for the Human Resource Management course.

Appendix D—Career and Technical Education Portfolio

Experiential Learning Portfolio

CIS 175—Introduction to Networking

Jonathan

Education History, Learning, and Goals Statement

As part of the ELP application, a draft outlining the students' educational history and goals is required, and I can see why this would be a requirement. This process of taking classes to complete a degree and evaluating my professional experience has been a learning and development process in itself. This draft below chronicles my 25-year continuing effort to complete a college degree and how my two decades of professional experience and continued learning has given me the fundamental learning components as they are aligned to the curriculum of my university I am seeking life experience credit for.

There is a separate technical essay included in this ELP application that demonstrates my knowledge and practical application of the subject matter in this course; however, I think that in the context of college it is more important to highlight how I learned the material. The learning process for me is quite easy to characterize in that I followed a crawl, walk, and run approach. My general attitude in life is that I am always learning and embracing learning new things and studying my craft to constantly improve my professional expertise.

While I did take the official Microsoft Windows NT 4.0 training classes (I held a Windows NT 4.0 MCSE and Microsoft Certified Trainer NT 4.0) I never took any Cisco official classes. Following my experiences getting military specialty training from the US Army (former Military Intelligence operator) and successfully completing the NT 4.0 MCSE training and certification, I was able to purchase the Juniper and Cisco books (and downloaded Cisco and Sonicwall documentation) and over time purchased a $20,000 networking lab composed of 30+ routers, switches, and firewalls of multiple vendors including Juniper, Cisco, HP, Adtran, and Sonicwall and learned the material on my own. (In the late 90s because of the instability of NT 4.0 and always dealing with server crashes, I felt that IP networking and security would be a better career path.)

My father taught me at a young age that in order to talk and think about any subject, I first had to learn the vocabulary. I started in chapter 1 of the Cisco and Juniper books and started by learning the fundamentals of networking and security (not just Cisco) and continuing through the chapters and completing the labs with the actual networking lab I built at home. I followed the book chapters and labs to completion. Working in IT I was assigned to projects and continued to learn in the field through hands on experience as well as being taught by colleagues senior to me. At times there were concepts I was not grasping completely on my own, and those are the times that I took advantage of senior colleagues to help me learn and ingest the concepts to complete comprehension. (This was before the day of YouTube and the advent of effective Internet-based distance learning. In the last few years I have embraced YouTube and other Internet educational subscriptions (i.e.—plurasight.com) to continue my learning of relevant subject matter.)

I have been doing IP networking and security professionally since 1997, and in that time I have personally configured, integrated, and trouble-shot over 1000 routers, switches, and firewalls/IPS systems in very complex topologies. On each project (complex and simple) I can say that I was always learning and sharpening my skill set. I find myself going back to the text books and vendor documentation and rereading sections during projects and gaining more understanding. On multiple occasions these national and global networks had to be secured to government compliance standards (including but not limited to CIP/NERC, SOX, SEC) which meant design and integration to high security standards that were audited for adherence to compliance requirements. In these cases it was not only important that I understood the networking and security technologies but I also had to learn and design/configure the systems to meet specific criteria. It was the implementation of these compliance requirements that made me realize that everything I learned was accurate as my clients were audited and never fined for any deficiencies.

During my career, I have also mentored others who I have worked with by constantly sharing my knowledge and experiences. I have colleagues all over the world that continue to call me to explain networking and security concepts to aid in their career progression. Out of all the classes in my bachelor's degree program, I am only applying for ELP for only four (4) classes Introduction to Networking, Network Security Fundamentals, Advanced Routing, and Internetwork Switching. These four classes are the core of what I have spent the last 18 years learning and cultivating of my skills. As I consider my learning in the context of 200, 300, and 400 level college courses, I would hope that a candidacy like this would typify the ELP program.

I have been working towards my college degree my entire adult life. My high school graduation was in 1991 and joined the US Army that summer. In 1993, I took my first college classes as a part-time student while I was a full-time soldier. After leaving the US Army, I took the MCSE curriculum, and after successful completion of that I started again with college classes at City College of New York (CCNY) to continue my efforts towards a bachelor's degree (this was while teaching myself IP networking, security, and virtualization and executing these skills on real world projects). I am excited at the prospect of finally completing my college degree and continuing on my efforts to study for the CISSP. With (hopefully) successful ELP application for these four (4) classes, I will be completing my degree next semester (Winter 2016). At that point, it would have taken me 25 years and the curriculum at my university makes me feel like I "earned my degree."

In this draft, I will take the opportunity to comment on the experience I had here at my university. I was drawn to my university for the ELP to capitalize on my previous learning and professional experience, but I have to say that the classes I had to take at my university to complete my program were really relevant to being an IT professional in the year 2015. I really saw the value in taking an HTML 5 class, and I actually enjoyed the CIS 210 Systems Analysis and Design class (among others). This makes me feel like a well-rounded technical professional. This program did increase my professional vocabulary at multiple levels, and this is valuable to me.

Included with this application are letters from professional colleagues whom I have worked closely with. I invite you to read those letters as beyond just stating that I know the subject matter of these classes, they highlight that I am always aiming to execute my professional responsibilities to the highest standards. With that said, the process of learning is perpetual for me. In the last few years I have started to teach myself the PowerShell language and it has had a dramatic impact on my skill set and I will continue to pursue technical training as well as certifications and likely an MBA (since I am also a business owner). Additionally and most notably I have started to integrate IPv6 into my designs and implementations (which includes getting my own IPv6 address space from the ARIN and subnetting it in my infrastructure). Just PowerShell and IPv6 alone can keep a technical professional learning for the next 10 years.

The learning process never stops for many personalities and there are those of us who embrace that. As I conclude this draft and ELP application I would like to think that this is the type of situation that the ELP was created for. I hope that this draft along with the rest of this application reflects a strong candidacy for ELP by illustrating that I have learned the materials to college-level proficiency and beyond and I thank my university for the opportunity to submit this application

Plagiarism Statement

Everything written in all associated documents with the ELP assessments comes from my pen, learning, and experience. The technical aspects written are my words after a 20 year education and career as a networking and security engineer from information I learned through independent study and in the field as well as exhaustive reading of vendor documentation Cisco Press, O'Reilly, and Sybex books in that time. I did not copy/paste anything into my application essays that is not my own writing or prior work experience.

*It is notable that in my CIS 275 class the professor questioned if my writing was my own because I did not use any references (when not required) and still produced comprehensive papers. I called my advisor and professor to explain the issue and then I was given full credit for all my work.

PLA Technical Narrative to Illustrate Learning and Comprehension of Course Materials

Abstract

Entering the IT industry in the mid 1990s has given this student the opportunity to grow with the explosion of the Internet. In 1995 I left the US Army Military Intelligence Corps (82nd Airborne Division) with the ambition to get my college degree and have a career as an IT professional. Since then I have been going to college at nights and on weekends while operating an IT consulting firm as the senior technologist based out of New York City with presence in Boulder, CO, and Los Angeles, CA, and clients all over the world. Additionally I have been flown all over the world multiple times by my clients to destinations including Singapore, Tokyo, London, Frankfurt, and Paris as well as domestic destinations all over the United States. This draft will demonstrate that my career responsibilities have led me to competencies that encompass the course learning outcomes of CIS 175—Introduction to Networking.

Computer networks are "the plumbing" of today's Internet-reliant global society. It is the responsibility of the network architects and engineers to design and deploy reliable and secure network topologies to support business critical applications as well as support governments, commerce, and consumer applications (i.e. Social Networking). This student has been given the opportunity to design and deploy global networks from a green field as well as conduct complex integration with existing infrastructure. This draft is the narrative of this student's interpretation of the course learning outcomes with a supported network diagram and command-line interface (CLI) scripts that would be used to deploy the network in accord with the diagram.

To compose the content of this essay I used the CIS 175 course syllabus published by my university and the only Table of Contents of the Sybex Network+ book and not the actual book contents. This was done to make sure I was able to account to all areas of knowledge that are required to illustrate. The details and the content of this essay are from what I learned and applied in real world projects.

Network administrators are taught the seven (7) layer Open Systems Interconnect (OSI) reference model (All People Seem To Need Data Processing or Application, Presentation Session, Transport, Network, Data Link, and Physical layers respectively) as well as DARPA and other models in the first week of classes because these models are the most fundamental construct for all communications between hosts on a network. This seven layer model provides application and hardware developers a frame work to develop solutions at specified levels in the stack and only have to talk to the adjacent levels (above and below) in order to integrate with the entire stack which makes integration less complex.

The OSI model does not only give application developers a construct but it also serves as this student's foundation for most network related trouble-shooting. After some time in the field (in my experience) network administrators start to put all problems and solutions into the context of the OSI model. In the context of CIS 175 this draft will focus on layers 1–3 (wiring, switching, and routing) and explore layers 4 (TCP/UDP) and 7 (application) for voice and QoS—in effect LANs, MANs, and voice optimized WANs.

In order to standardize network communications across the global community the IEEE (Institute of Electrical and Electronic Engineers—a.k.a—the "I triple-E") which governs standards and protocols across many technologies also developed standards and protocols for all network vendors and manufacturers to comply with. For many of these technologies we see something like "802.#" with the # being the variable of that standards nomenclature. By doing this there can be vendors and manufacturers all over the world that make systems that can talk to each other.

The first layer of the OSI model is the physical layer which means this is "where everything plugs in" also known as "physical media." The most common cable is the Ethernet RJ-45 twisted pair cable with four copper wiring pairs that is "pinned out" for Ethernet. This is the type of wire that connected most networking gear around the world. CAT-5 has a maximum speed of 1 GbE (can also support 10/100Base-T @ 10/100 MBPS) and CAT-6 can support up to 10 GbE and can go a few hundred feet. (Legacy CAT-3 can only support 10 MBPS is used in older voice installations in the 1980's and 90's also has RJ-11 ends sometimes but still the same media as CAT-3 with RJ-45.) Most late model switches support RJ-45 connected to twisted pair. ("Straight though" cables typically support connection between hosts and switches but something called a "cross-over cable" which uses the same twisted pair but pinned to both ends match and is used to connect PCs directly to each other as well as switches directly to each other. New technology called AIX removed the need for cross-over cables for connecting devices directly to each other.) For higher speed communication and communication over long distances with low latency single mode fiber (SMF) optic technology is used. Multimode fiber (MMF) also exists and is used across shorter distances than SMF. Fiber media consists of the fiber cable itself and then devices call SFPs that go on each end of the fiber that is the appropriate SFP for the fiber cable and the fiber switch it connects to. Another legacy media is called coaxial cable that can transmit at 10 MBPS (10Base-2) which is a copper cable that connects with ends called British Navel Connectors (BNC). Even though copper, fiber, and coax are different (layer-1) physical media they all support Ethernet at layer-2 with the appropriate connections and can even be made to talk to each other with media converters as well as routers. Data is put on the wire in layer-1 as PDUs called bits. For connected Ethernet ports, speed and duplex setting have to be negotiated by the switch port and connected host. Speed is usually with 10, 100, or 1000 MBPS while duplex is either half-duplex or full-duplex.

A port in half-duplex can either send or receive at any one time while a port in full-duplex can send and receive at the same time—*this is important for voice and video connected interfaces. (It is interesting to note that physical media between a demarc for a T-1 and the CSU/DSU in the T-1 card (WIC) in the router uses a cable that is pinned out for Ethernet and has RJ-45 connections on each side but the connection between the demark and WIC is NOT Ethernet.)

Skipping to layer-3 of the OSI reference model in which PDUs are called packets. When thinking about the concept of networking this student first thinks of an "IP address." An IP address is a logical address that is 32 bits in length (four octets of eight bits each). Each IP address consists of two parts; a network address and a host address. A "subnet mask" is used to separate the network portion of the IP address from the host portion. An example of an IPv4 address and subnet mask in numeric format would be 192.168.1.1/255.255.255.0 (or 192.168.1.1/24 because a 255.255.255.0 subnet mask illustrates 24 bits). It is important to note that while network administrators see and use numbering, the computer system translates that numbered IP address into binary so the IP address 192.168.1.1/24 would be 11000000.10101000.00000001.00000001/11111111.11111111.11111 111.0 in binary. When sending packets to a remote IP host, the sending host compares the destination IP address with its local IP address and subnet to see if the destination is on the same network. If the receiving host is on a remote subnet, then the packet is forwarded to a default-gateway or designated route out of the appropriate exit interface. (A layer-3 broadcast is 255.255.255.255 of "all 1's" 11111111.1111111.11111111.11111111.)

The IP addressing system is the routed protocol used globally to support internetworking between hosts systems and the Internet. The version being used since its inception is IPv4 which is a 32 bit address but has a limitation of 4 billion plus "public" IP addresses. (The term public IP address means a valid address that is routable across the public Internet. There are three ranges in the RFC 1918 that are not legitimate addresses and used behind firewalls in private networks. The ranges are 10.0.0.0/8, 172.16.0.0/20, and 192.168.0.0/24. These are referred to as "private" IP addresses.) Because of the limitation of IPv4 addresses network designers use a mechanism called Network Address Translation (NAT) which gives organizations connected to the Internet to have a single public IP address shared by the entire private network. It is notable that IPv4 is hierarchical and has "classes" of addresses based on the first three bits of the IP address. Class A, B, and C are for general production and class D addresses are used for networking services. A set of addresses called "multicast" addresses from ranges 224.0.0.0 to 239. 0.0.0 allow one-to-many communications between multiple IP addresses while typical unicast IP address are communication between only two IP addresses. Multicasting is helpful for delivering the same streaming media content to multiple nodes at the same time from a single source. Class A, B, and C networks can be subnetted hierarchically; however, with the advent of Classless Internet Domain Routing (CIDR) networks are viewed as independent IP spaces in the global routing table instead of the hierarchal structure of the three classes of production networks. The process of subnetting is borrowing bits from the host portion of the IP address and lending them to the network portion. This extends the subnet mask and network address and shortens the available host bits. So while there are more networks available there are less hosts bits available on each network. Not every network is subnetted the same way for contiguously. Network designs can create subnets of different sizes using different subnet mask length which is called variable length subnet masking (VLSM). Subnetted networks can only talk to each other through a router that has routes to both subnets. These subnets do not have to be contiguous, but for subnets that are contiguous that are behind the same router a network administrator has the options of summarizing or supernetting those subnets to a single subnet with a shorter subnet mask.

With the IPv4 address space depleting and requirement for Internet connectivity is only growing. Internet engineers have commissioned a new version of IP which is called IPv6. The new IPv6 addressing is already being implemented by governments and private organizations and is a

128 bit address that has an innumerable amount of addresses available (more addresses than the human race could ever use). Since IPv4 and IPv6 will be running parallel for the next few decades there are multiple technologies to support this including but not limited to dual-stack (running IPv4 and IPv6 addressing on the same interfaces) as well as 6to4 tunneling which encapsulates IPv6 packets across and IPv4 WAN.

IPv6 addresses are a bit more complex and (as mentioned above) are 128 bits in length. An IPv6 address has three parts—a global prefix, a subnet, and then a host. And similar to IPv4 there is a set of "private IP addresses" in IPv6 called local-link and unique addresses that are not meant to be routed over the public Internet. But since there are so many public IPv6 addresses available, in many cases public networks are subnetted and placed behind a firewall without the need for NAT. An example of an IPv6 address would be 2001:abcd:0000:0000:0000:0000:1234:5678 and can be written as 2001:abcd:0:0:0:0:1234:5678 because IPv6 gives the options to collapse four zeroes to one zero and can do that on contiguous octets of all zeros. IPv6 does not have multi-cast addressing support but does have Anycast which is not the same but similar outcomes. An Anycast address is a single IP address assigned to multiple network adapters (sometimes called one-to-many).

TCP/IP is a layer-3 "routed protocol" that applies logical addressing to hosts on a network. As already mentioned TCP/IP addresses are assigned to hosts and host addresses are assigned to "networks." Networks and subnetworks (subnets) are contiguous addresses within the same binary subnet mask. Subnets are smaller networks that have been "subnetted" from larger networks. The term *subnetted* implies the breaking apart of a large network into smaller networks. A router can tell what network it is on based on the assigned IP address and subnet mask of an interface. As long as that interface is enabled, that network will be in the local routing table of that router as a "connected" route. Consequentially any IP address and mask assigned to any enabled interface on the router will populate that local routing table with the respective network and know which network can be reached from which interface. Two routers connected to each other will typically have interfaces on the same subnet; therefore, any networks connected to each respective routers would be reachable from any interface on both routers across that inter-router connection. Reachability between routes connected to each respective router is facilitated through a route in each router stating that the destination networks reachable through a router should be sent from the source router out of the connected interface to the destination router (and the destination router MUST have the routes going in the opposite direction as well). In simple topologies these routes can be populated into each route manually called a static route. If router A had IP addresses 192.168.1.1/24 and 192.168.2.1/24 and router B has IP addresses 192.168.2.254/24 and 192.168.3.1/24 then router A would have a static route "ip route 192.168.3.0 255.255.255.0 192.168.2.254" and router B would have a static route "ip route 192.168.1.0 255.255.255.0 192.168.2.1" to facilitate routing of TCP/IP between hosts on the internetwork of two routers. Further down in the draft "dynamic routing" is explored in the context of reliability but dynamic routing protocols such as RIP, EIGRP, OSFP, and BGP can be used for scalability by routers to tell their peer routers about networks they are connected to and know about through other routers. (*Note the difference that TCP/IP is a "routed" protocol while RIP, EIGRP, OSFP and BGP are "routing" protocols.) If we were to consider a network of 100+ routers and 250+ networks it is not practical for a network administrator to enter and maintain hundreds of routes across hundreds of routers using static routes. Each router exchanges its routing table with destination networks and respective egress interfaces with the adjacent routers configured with the same routing proto-col and similar parameters (i.e.—area number, autonomous system number, etc...). RIP and BGP are distance vector protocols that weigh routes based on hops (RIP uses IP network hops as the distance and BGP uses autonomous system number hops as the distance). OSPF and ISIS are link state protocols that use link speeds to calculate weight of routes so OSPF will look at three hops each with a 100 MBPS link as a better route than two hops each with a 1.544 MBPS (T-1) links when evaluating the better path if multiple paths to the same destination are available. EIGRP is a hybrid routing protocol that uses bandwidth, delay, and reliability (by default) to evaluate routes. These routing protocols support IPv4 and have been updated to support IPv6.

In the current age it should be mentioned that firewalls and layer-3 switches (in addition to routers) are layer-3 devices that have IP addresses on multiple subnets and participate in static and dynamic routing for IP reachability. (IP reachability in the firewall is not the same as IP accessibility in that even though a firewall knows how to route the traffic between interfaces it will not pass the traffic unless it has a rule (or access control list (ACL)) allowing that traffic. This does not account for transparent firewalls.)

An IPv4 address can be assigned to a host in two ways called "static" IP addresses and "dynamic" IP addresses. A static IP address is a predetermined address assigned to a host by a network administrator. This is usually done with servers, printers, routers, and firewalls. It is not practical to manually assign static IP addresses to hundreds of workstations in an enterprise so to solve this issue there is a protocol called Dynamic Host Configuration Protocol (DHCP) which assigns IP addresses/masks to hosts dynamically out of a pool from a DHCP server. The DHCP server can also assign advanced IP address parameters such as DNS servers and default-gateways. If a Windows host is set to be a DHCP client and there is no DHCP server available, then an address on the 169.254.x.x/16 APIPA (automatic private IP addressing) network is randomly assigned by the hosts. All hosts in the same collision domain on the 169.154 network can talk to each other. IPv6 has multiple options for dynamically assigning IP addresses which includes DHCP (similar to IPv4) and "stateless autoconfiguration" (EUI-64). This learns the global prefix and subnet ID from the router as the first part of the address and then a field with :FFFE: then the 48 bit MAC address of the interface.

Between layers 1 and 3 of the OSI referenced model is layer 2 known as the data link layer and media access control layer in which PDUs are called frames. This essay will focus most on Ethernet as the layer-2 protocol which uses a 48 bit MAC (media access control) address that is a physical address "burned into" a network adapter. No single MAC address appears twice on Earth (unless it is virtual). The first part of the MAC address is the burned in component that is a string assigned to a vendor (such as Broadcom or Intel) while the rest of the address is a unique string to that vendor. The IEEE construct makes sure that the same MAC address is not used between multiple vendors.

Local Area Networks can be built in multiple topologies such as bus, star, ring, and mesh. This essay will focus mostly on the Ethernet bus topology which has all hosts on a broadcast domain talking to each other. Older topologies, like star which has all nodes talking through a central node, ring which has a logical ring between all hosts, and mesh which has physical connections between all connected devices, are used less in newer deployments because they are not as flexible and reliable as the bus topology provided by Ethernet. It should be noted that Ethernet has components that make it flexible and reliable. When considering Ethernet hardware the first thing to understand is the process of putting data on the wire and contention and the differences between an Ethernet hub and an Ethernet switch. Ethernet has something called a collision domain in that within a collision domain only a single host can put a frame on the wire at any given time. A protocol known as carrier sense multiple access with collision detection (CDMA/CD) which senses PDU interactions on the bus and sends when appropriate as well as responding appropriately when collisions occur and retransmission of PDUs in the appropriate intervals. With a hub all ports are a single collision domain and therefore only one port can transmit at any given time which each port on a switch is its own collision domain and therefore all hosts connected to each respective port can transmit independent of other port activity. Broadcast domains at layer-2 are defined as VLAN (virtual LANs), and each port on a switch that is assigned to a VLAN is on that VLANs broadcast domain. So VLANs in a single switch can partition that single switch into multiple virtual segments to break up traffic between broadcast domains. (Historically, broadcast domains are broken up by routers, layer-3 switches, and firewalls.) A device on any port in the same broadcast domain can send traffic to any other port in that same broadcast domain. A broadcast MAC address would be 48 bits of "all F's."

Switch ports that have single hosts (such as a workstation or server) connected to them are known as "access ports" in the Cisco platform and "untagged" ports in other IEEE supported platforms. This means that a single access port belongs to a single VLAN. In many environments ports are assigned to VLANs statically, but there are environments that support dynamic VLANs based on criteria (such as MAC address of username in 802.1x). However, a switch with multiple VLANs might need to uplink to other switches with multiple VLANs to extend the broadcast domain throughout multiple floors in a building or over a campus. On the Cisco platform these uplink ports between switches are called "trunks" and on other IEEE platforms traffic sent on these ports is called "tagged." The terminology of tagged and untagged comes from the IEEE protocol known as 802.1Q (a.k.a—dot1q) which adds a VLAN "tag" in the PDU for all tagged traffic.

The Local Area Network (a.k.a—the LAN) is the smallest topology that can be considered to be a "high speed network" whether connected by a cross-over cable or through an Ethernet switch/hub. (This draft will focus most on the Ethernet LAN topology as it is the most prevalent in today's deployment models.) A LAN is one or multiple broadcast domains (or VLANs) connected by a high-speed hub or switch (1 GbE, 10 GbE, 40 GbE, etc...). It is notable that a switch not only separates broadcast domains with VLANs but also makes each port a collision domain unlike a hub which has a common collision domain for all ports. In many deployments a "layer-3" switch is used to facilitate communications between broadcast domains with inter-VLAN routing (the switch has to have the correct licensing to support this layer-3 functionality). A common topology for a small business with a single location might be the deployment of four VLANs inside the firewall (voice, workstations, secure wireless, and servers), one server DMZ VLAN, one guest wireless DMZ VLAN, and two Internet VLANs outside the firewall (one for each ISP respectively in a dual-ISP topology) for a total of eight (8) VLANs. Cisco has a proprietary protocol called Virtual Trunking Protocol that shares VLANs between multiple switches. All VLANs are created only on VTP servers (server mode), and then VTP clients (client mode) get the updated VLAN list from the servers. There is a VTP mode called transparent and does not use VTP information to populate the local VLAN list but will pass VTP data through to connected switches. Transparent mode is required for using more than 1024 VLANs. I usually either disable VTP for security because it is unnecessary or place the switch in VTP transparent mode because a switch that comes on line as a server with a bad VLAN topology and a high priority number can remove valid VLANs from VTP client and server switches. To that point, never leave VTP in the default configuration of server with no domain and no password.

Edge power-over-Ethernet switch ports that have connected IP phones with a tethered workstation provide power to the connected IP phone and require a special port configuration that sends the workstation traffic "through" the phone untagged and voice VLAN traffic "to" the phone tagged and recognized by the VoIP phone internal switch. The phone must either have the voice VLAN tagged in the configuration or get the tag from the switch via CDP (Cisco Discovery Protocol) or LLDP-MED.

*It is important to note that ALL communication between hosts on an Ethernet LAN is done between MAC addresses at layer-2 even when the network administrator sends a PING between the IP addresses. The hosts use ARP entries (Address Resolution Protocol) to resolve the layer-3 IP addresses to the layer-2 MAC addresses to identify the correct forwarding switch port.

An extension of the wired LAN that uses physical switches and CAT-5 cabling to connect computers to the network is the wireless LAN (WLAN—a.k.a WiFi). Most people will recognize the numbers 802.11a/b/g/Wireless-N running at ranges of 2.4 GHz and 5 GHz, and each has notable strength, range, and reception metrics associated. 802.11 has been known by the IEEE as the protocols for WiFi communications. A service set ID (SSID) is the basic wireless network that can be secured by protocols such as WEP (old) and WPA2 (usually a key has to be entered in order to gain access to a WPA2 network). A device with a WiFi antenna that provides WiFi access to clients is usually called a wireless access point (WAP). Advanced WALs can support multiple SSIDs and 802.1q trunking and multiple VLANs. WiFi is mostly layer-2, switched networking that uses SSIDs mapped to VLANs to separate WLANs. A good idea is to make separate SSIDs for traffic inside the firewall and placing a guest SSID outside the firewall. WiFi networks do have two notable types, which are "ad hoc" and "infrastructure." An ad hoc WLAN is like having two wired devices connected with a cross-over cable, and those devices can only communicate with each other. In contrast an infrastructure topology is similar to a broadcast domain on a wired switch in which all hosts can talk to each other. Simple WiFi deployments can have a single WAP which is easy to manage; however, when a topology becomes more complex adding multiple WAPs throughout a building, a campus, or even a Wide Area Network, it then becomes more difficult to manage many WAPs individually which then calls for a device known as WLAN controller. After a WAP is registered with a controller, it can be managed through a central location making it easier for an administrator to update policies across all WAPs in an enterprise. Another (cool) thing that controllers can do is enable clients roaming between WAPs without losing connections (two independent WAPs each with the same SSIDs does not support roaming and would not give the end user the best experience while roaming though a controller controlled wireless infrastructure provides a more contiguous end user wireless experience). *It should be noted that when using multiple WAPs in a confined area that the frequencies need to be configured not to cancel each other out. This is something else that a WLAN controller can help manage.

Most new model PCs, Macs, and printers have built in wireless network adapters as well as a wired network adapter, which gives the hosts the ability to gain access to LAN and WLAN when either is available. There is not much thought given the client side LAN and WLAN network interface cards (NICs); however, an integrator does need to consider type of WAPs being used on a WLAN deployment. A wireless network needs to consider how many clients will connect to it, their physical ranges, and required bandwidth. In order to completely cover areas to meet expectations, it is many times necessary to conduct a site survey and choose the number of WAPs with the appropriate antenna strength.

While LAN topologies are usually a single location or campus and support high speed communications between the hosts, for short distances a Metro Area Network (MAN) can be used to inter-connect LANs at high-speeds at layer-2 without dark fiber. A Wide Area Network (WAN) is required to facilitate layer-3 IP communications across long distances. (This student has implemented global layer-2 VPLS WANs but will keep the scope of this draft limited to layer-3 WANs.) To support a WAN link a "router" is used. Historically, routers were used not only to route packets between IP networks but also to route between media types such as a DS-3 WAN connection to an Ethernet LAN connection.

In the past WANs have been associated with private circuits between two or more locations connected by dedicated routers; however, as technologies have evolved to keep pace with business needs, an alternate WAN topology called VPN (virtual private network) has become quite prevalent that sends private data in encrypted format across the public Internet. While this type of WAN does not support end-to-end QoS, it does provider a cheaper solution than leased-lines if voice and video is not a requirement. VPN can be used to securely connect two or more locations as well as being used by telecommuters to securely access private information from the untrusted, public Internet. The way the VPN supports secure communications between private networks over the Internet is through the use of an encrypted VPN tunnel. Most firewalls also act as a local VPN concentrator that terminates each end of a site-to-site VPN. The outside public IP address of each firewall form an encrypted tunnel using a suite of protocols called IPSec. Each firewall is configured to know about the firewall on the other side with parameters such as remote IP address, pre-shared key (if not using certificates), remote subnets, and phase 1 and phase 2 hash and encryption algorithms. Phase 1 establishes secure ISAKMP communications between the two VPN peers with agreed on protocols (i.e.—MD5/3DES) then the firewall peers will have a secure connection and can then exchange pre-shared keys. The phase 2 builds the actual IPSec tunnel after the protocols (i.e.—SHA-1/AES-256) are agreed on and interesting source and destination traffic is matched up. Most VPN platforms integrate the IPSec tunnels with dynamic routing protocols for enterprise scalability. A site-to-site VPN is topologically very similar to a routed connection but without QoS.

Another type of VPN (in addition to site-to-site) is called remote access (RA) VPN. RA is for users who are working outside the firewall at a remote site and require secure access to resources inside the firewall. The firewall/VPN concentrator is configured to receive RA connections (either with IPSec of SSL) and grant access to the appropriate resource behind the firewall based on the RA policy applied to that user. An example is that an internal user to a company will have access to IP addresses of many of the servers while a vendor RA policy will only allow access to designated servers that are specific to a TCP/UDP port. After the VPN concentrator is configured, the IPSec or SSL client software is installed on the remote host (Windows, Mac, and Linux clients) and configured with the public IP address (or FQDN) of the concentrator to establish communications. The RA user is first authenticated onto the RA VPN by means of user name and password and possibly even a one-time password from a two-factor authentication fob. The user name is evaluated again and access-list and assigned access to the appropriate resources based on the RA policy. Similar to site-to-site VPNs, RA VPNs do not support QoS either. This is because traffic across the public Internet does not recognize QoS tags.

Since WANs connect multiple locations together, they are usually looked at as either point-to-point topology in which two locations are connected to each other with a dedicated circuit between them. A point-to-multipoint topology is a topology in which a WAN communication media, such as frame-relay or MPLS, can connect two more locations directly to each other with a single WAN link at each site (respectively). Site–to-site VPNs can be built to support fullmesh/point-to-multipoint or a hub and spoke topology depending on the preferences of the VPN network designed based on the requirements. In contrast with point-to-point topologies, sites can only communicate with sites they are directly connected to or through a hub site. A full mesh of point-to-point circuits would require N*(N-1) total WAN connections.

Since TCP traffic at layer-4 (session layer – TCP = Transmission Control Protocol) of the OSI reference model is connection oriented and requires acknowledgement of each packet sent, there are two specific problems that happen on a WAN that do not (or should not) happen on a well-managed WAN. These problems are latency and limited bandwidth causing poor user experience. Latency is a problem (regardless of bandwidth) that has its source as the limitation of the speed of light. For a packet to go from NYC to Tokyo and back takes about 300 milliseconds (or about 1/3rd of a second). Notwithstanding sliding windows a basic TCP conversation between two hosts across a WAN is such that the sending host will send a 64k chunk across the WAN and wait for an ACK before sending the next 64k chunk. So it has to wait about 1/3rd of a second between each 64k chunk, which translates to days/weeks/months when the scope becomes moving terabytes of data. As with the advent of global WANs and commerce there are solutions for these problems called WAN optimizers. These technologies act as a local TCP proxy to the LAN hosts and manage the WAN connection through techniques like WAN deduplication (among other proprietary algorithms). Applications that use connectionless UDP (User Datagram Protocol—like voice and video) are not impacted by distance like TCP is because no ACK is required; however, bandwidth congestion can most certainly impact voice and video performance (as explained below with QoS).

This student would like to make note that the broad use of WAN optimization technologies has added new dimensions of complexity when trouble-shooting WAN topology issues because these technologies (above just honoring and confirm QoS) actually change the packets and take action on them as they traverse the appliance. An example would be that a PING and TRACEROUTE work just fine, but a CIFS connection cannot be established over the WAN.

The second problem specific to WANs (and not as much LANs) is the limited bandwidth. While LAN switches are 10/40 GbE between the servers and 1 GbE at the user access, the WAN connection might only be 50 MBPS. The WAN then becomes the "bottleneck" as more data is trying to be forced through the WAN contention will occur for WAN bandwidth (consider traffic going from 1000 lanes down to 50 lanes during rush hour, which gives rise to the question of getting ambulances through these bottlenecks and not getting held up for hours). A network administrator has to make sure that their SSH management access to the network equipment is never squashed out by a file copy; however, a more user facing application is voice which has other considerations. Voice is a real time application that requires packets to be delivered together AND in sequence. An optimized LAN/MAN/WAN supports end-to-end Quality-of- Service (QoS) to maintain the integrity of the real time voice traffic as it traverses the LAN/WAN. End-to-End QoS starts at the access (edge) switch when the ingress port identifies the COS or DSCP tag. The tag is then honored as it traverses the LAN fabric. Once the voice or video packet is at the provider facing WAN interface, a well-managed WAN will have an egress policy that identifies the voice traffic and puts it into the correct queue for order and prioritization as the packets are put onto the WAN media with limited bandwidth. (Notable that voice traffic is UDP and therefore does not require an ACK for each packet, WAN latency can be an issue but TCP WAN optimizers cannot solve this problem for voice.)

Another type of reliability of a network is redundancy, and redundancy comes at multiple levels and supported by multiple protocols. For WAN and route redundancies there are dynamic IP routing protocols like RIP, ISIS, OSPF, EIGRP, and BGP (among others). These dynamic routing protocols share network topology routes between routers participating in dynamic routing and can detect network route failures and update the routing tables in the participating WAN routers of the appropriate link to reach their destination. During regular operation with multiple paths, the router will select the path with the lower administrative distance and when a route fails, the router will remove that route to the destination from the routing table and then take the alternate path. The respective administrative distances for routing are AD of 1 for static routes, BGP has an AD of 20, EIGRP has an AD of 90, OSPF has an AD of 110, and RIP has an AD of 120.

On the LAN side there are much more strict rules to maintaining redundant links. Unlike in routing where multiple active paths can exist between source/destination, in a switching environment (not including port-channel) there cannot be multiple active links between source and destination hosts. This does not, however, impede the ability to have redundant links. Layer-2 fabrics use Spanning-Tree Protocol to maintain a list of all links in the topology and best paths to the root bridges (by sharing BPDUs) while keeping redundant links from forwarding packets until necessary. An STP network that has all switches connected and all links accounted for is considered to be "fully converged." Similar to routing protocols, there are multiple flavors of STP (i.e.—Rapid Spanning Tree Protocol—RSTP) and each version of STP has means of setting the priorities for preferred links over non-preferred links. Important to note that different flavors of STP have different names for STP port states with the fundamental states of native STP being blocking, listening, learning, and forwarding. While routes are weighed in "administrative distances," STP LAN links are weighed in "costs." A Spanning-Tree domain has a "root bridge," and what STP basically does is calculate lowest costs from all switches paths to the root bridge with the use of root ports (ports closest to the root) and designated ports in the fabric. The topology converges automatically, but a network administrator can set the costs between switches and the root manually on the configuration of the uplink ports by entering a higher cost on the link. It is true that in STP prevents loops by shutting down additional layer-2 links there is a technology call "port-channel" that binds two–eight physical switch ports to a single logical port-channel that supports aggregated bandwidth for all participating ports as well as redundancy for a failed port. (A single traffic flow through a port-channel cannot exceed the bandwidth of a single port in the port-channel as more connections form the bandwidth from additional ports in the port-channel is used. STP recognizes all the switch ports in a single port-channel as one logical port and assigns a cost to the entire port-channel and not to the individual ports in the port-channel.)

While security is not the first paragraph in this essay, it should be the first consideration when designing and deploying any network. Attacks come from all different directions that can originate from a computer out on the public Internet outside the firewall or a host inside the firewall that has been compromised and exploited by a virus or malware. IT organizations should work under that premise that everything is unsafe and restrict everything (within reason); then, after evaluating user requirements and risk factors resources will be allowed access to. This is when "access control" starts getting addressed. Different tools are used to detect and thwart different threats.

All security starts with physical security and making sure critical network components are locked in a room with sufficient power and HVAC. Access control to the room should be monitored. An optimal security posture minimizes the size of the attack footprint by disabling unnecessary services and also applies security to all services where possible/feasible. Starting with connecting to the appliance for management—the networking equipment should be in a locked room. Usernames and passwords should exist in the networking gear and stored in encrypted format. For remote management of the networking gear, it should be locked down with an access-list and only secure protocols that support encryption, such as SSH and HTTPS, should be used instead of telnet and http which send data in clear-text. If routing protocols are employed, they too should be hardened with MD5 authentication and only active on participating interfaces. Further control-plane security can be applied to edge devices to help avoid malicious attacks like DDoS attacks that overwhelm the network control-plane with denied requests (among other attack vectors available to hackers).

Above encrypted management protocols and a hardened control-plane, access control to the network gear is managed by a suite of protocols called AAA ("triple A"), which stands for network authentication, authorization, and accounting that in most cases is facilitated by a NAC (network access control system). Authentication simply refers to granting access to a network resource based on a username and password. That username and password can be stored locally in the device or on a central system (such as an Active Directory Windows Server) that maintains the user list that all routers, switches, and firewall send login requests to. These requests are usually sent in a secure format called RADIUS (remote access dial up services) or LDAP which is a protocol native to Microsoft. Once the username and password is accepted, then access is granted to authorized resources. Not everyone logging into the network and all administrators will have the same level of access to the same resources. Authorization systems assign access policies based on user and group enrollment. Users are placed in the specific access groups to get appropriate access to the necessary resources. Accounting for changes in the network is required by many secure enterprises. An accounting system (such as Cisco ICE) not only keeps track of all users logged in but (among other things) keeps track of all the changes each user made. AAA services are used to control access to managing network systems as well as for managing access control to RA VPNs as well.

The layer-2 network has multiple layers of security to capitalize on to prevent other types of attacks like rogue DHCP servers, IP address spoofing, MAC address spoofing, and port-security. Port security can make sure that only a single or limited number of MAC addresses can send data through a given port. DHCP snooping identifies the ports that DHCP servers are connected to and only allows those ports to received DHCP discover and request packets while all other switch ports will drop all DHCP related packets from being received. IP and MAC address spoofing are different in that a malicious host is either trying to impersonate the IP or MAC address in question (like a server) so all traffic will go to the interloping host instead of the actual host. Switches with advanced security features can keep a map of every IP to MAC address resolution and correlate to the port it is designated for. If the switch receives a packet with a MAC address or IP address that does not match the port it is supposed to be, the switch will drop the packet and not forward it. Another component of layer-2 security is preventing "VLAN hopping" across trunks on the default, native VLAN. It is best practice to configure every trunk link between switches with an (untagged) native VLAN that is on the BLACKHOLE VLAN (the BLACKHOLE VLAN is a VLAN that has not production ports assigned and all unused parts are assigned to that VLAN as part of general hardening).

For advanced analysis of traffic, a network administrator can run a packet capture which captures all the traffic going in/out of an interface and saves all the packet information to a .cap file that can be viewed in a protocol analyzer like WireShark (formerly known as Ethereal). WireShark can view the content of attributes of each packet in great detail and give much information for problem solving. (Interesting to note that managed switches can do something call port-mirroring for SPAN which can send a copy of all traffic in/out of a designated switch port to another port on the switch that has the computer running WireShark connected. So in that time, the WireShark computer is receiving a copy of all traffic; however, that destination port of the SPAN can only receive traffic from the SPAN and cannot send or receive any other traffic.)

Above a hardened security posture it is also recommended to implement all technologies in accordance with best-business-practices with respect to the technology and the vendor. For this reason it is important to review the documentation and release notes prior to taking any new devices live into production. This will ensure the implementation meets all industry and vendor requiem's and give a library for trouble-shooting commands and matrix.

As mentioned earlier an advanced security appliance called a network based "firewall" has become the norm to have installed at the boundary between a public Internet connection and a private network to maintain access control from the Internet in. A simple firewall would have an "outside" interface and an "inside" interface. The outside interface is considered to be the lowest security interface while the inside interface is the highest security interface. And most times by default ALL traffic hitting the outside interface is blocked unless there is a specific rule to apply certain types of traffic in (like traffic from anywhere on TCP ports 80 and 443 (HTTP and SSL) to a web server and traffic on TCP ports 25 and 993 (SMTP and IMAP) to a mail server behind the firewall). In contrast, all traffic going from the inside interface out allows all traffic by default giving hosts inside the firewall access to browse all remote IP subnets on the public Internet. Advanced firewall configurations might have another interface called a demilitarized zone (DMZ) which is between the inside and outside interfaces. In many cases, a DMZ is a place to put server's access from the public Internet that (for security reasons) a network administrator would not want to put "inside the firewall." In many cases traffic can pass from the inside interface to the DMZ and outside interfaces with no blocking while traffic from the DMZ can pass to the outside interface but is blocked from sending traffic into the inside of the firewall.

Most firewalls also provide a function call Network Address Translation (NAT) and Port Address Translation (PAT). PAT provides organizations with many computers inside the firewall on private networks with non-RFC 1918 private addressing the ability to have all privately addressed hosts browse the public Internet using a single public IP address. What PAT does is replace the source host private IP address (a.k.a—inside local) in the packet header with the public IP of the outside interface of the firewall (a.k.a.—outside local) on the egress. So the public web server (a.k.a—outside global address) receiving the request will see and respond to the public IP address of the firewall. NAT in many cases is about mapping a single public IP address to a single private IP address also called a one-to-one NAT. (Newer firewalls support one-to-many and many-to-one NATs, but this essay will focus on the one-to-one NAT). If there are multiple servers hosting public services (such as web and mail servers) it is likely the case that each server will have a private (inside local) IP address on the LAN and a public (outside local) IP address known by the public Internet. When the firewall receives the packets on the outside interface with the destination of a public (outside local) address that has an associated inside local NAT address, the firewall will translate that packet and forward the packet to the inside local host IP address. (*It is very important to note that NATting the traffic to the public server is not actually allowing the traffic. In addition to the NAT, the firewall must also have a rule that allows traffic (such as SSL and SMTP) to the outside local address has to be in place for the traffic to traverse the firewall.)

Many firewalls also have embedded Intrusion Prevention Systems (IPS). While a basic firewall allows and blocks traffic by source/destination IP address and TCP/UDP port, an IPS system looks at patterns. An example of a pattern that an IPS can see might be many failed attempts to log into a server behind the firewall with a bad username and password. The firewall allows the traffic, but an IPS would recognize this as a brute force address and automatically shun that source IP address from any traffic going to the firewall. An IPS can also pickup things like port scans and also shun those source addresses. IPS engines have databases of known signatures of dubious traffic types and as threats evolve IPS vendors make signature updates that are automatically downloaded to the IPS from the Internet (with paid subscription to vendor).

Above, this essay has detailed ways to secure the networks routers and switches as well as securing the network with a network based firewall. Separate from securing the plumbing of the network (routers, switches, and firewalls) it is just as important to secure the host systems with vulnerable operating systems such as Windows, Mac, and Linux hosts. The most fundamental security measure is to keep OS's running with the most current updates and security patches. Additionally, computer administrators will also install a software firewall, software anti-virus, and anti-malware services as well as DNS sanitization services. Taking these measures can help prevent a computer from becoming compromised and also find and clean infected computers. Microsoft Windows has a host based firewall as part of the OS as well as a free anti-virus engine called Windows Defender, and these can be used in conjunction with third-party security software agents. It is important to keep the heuristic engines of the respective anti-X components up to date. In most platforms the latest signatures are downloaded automatically every day and installed.

After a network is built, it has to be maintained and sometimes trouble-shooting performed. Over the years, networks and network devices have evolved to provide administrators with robust software and hardware tools and diagnostics for good network awareness. While tools like ICMP (PING) and TRACEROUTE exist to verify host and path connectivity, they alone do not provide historical views over periods of time. Tools like syslog and SNMP v3 can send encrypted messages (in the form of traps) with hardware and software specific MIBs (attributes) to a central repository for aggregation and view of SMNP messages from all devices. This can be done in tandem with basic network logging facilities as well as real-time "show" commands to get a complete picture (like show ARP—if you try to PING a Windows Server with the default firewall on settings the PING will time out. This may look like the host is down, but if you send a PING and it times out (from a host on the same subnet) you can then show the ARP table and see if there is a MAC address for that IP address. If there is an ARP entry with MAC and IP it is likely that the host is up but the firewall is on).

It should be noted that there is also trouble-shooting performed at the application layer done by the host computer (i.e.—Windows and Linux hosts). In addition to PING (and PATHPING) and TRACEROUTE, a diagnostic command that is useful for Internet browsing is called "NSLOOKUP." The NSLOOKUP command tests to see if a fully qualified domain name (FQDN) address can be resolved to an IP address by a designated DNS server successfully or not. Many times when a device cannot access the Internet, it may not be the IP routing as the issue but the ability to resolve the FQDN to IP address and the NSLOOKUP command is a diagnostic for this. Another command called NETSTAT illustrates IP and port connections that a host currently has open sessions to. NBTSTAT gives NETSTAT type statistics and address NetBIOS naming options to the output. The most used Windows IP diagnostic command is IPCONFIG which displays the IP configuration of the Windows host, and it should also be noted that NETSTAT, NBTSTAT, and IPCONFIG have switches and arguments following the commands to further specify the diagnostics.

The software tools mentioned above are very helpful in diagnosing logic and configuration issues, but sometimes it requires the use of physical tools to run diagnostics on the network wiring infrastructure. These tools include (but are not limited to) loopbacks, line testers, multi-meters, tone probes, as well as special tools for testing fiber optics. Each of the items mentioned performs specific testing on interfaces, structured wiring, voltages, and light paths (for fiber). Each tool is used at the appropriate time to help diagnose the issue at hand.

In the process of composing multiple essays to illustrate mastery of networking concepts, this student also realized that the process of learning and evolving never stops throughout an entire career. There are industry professionals across multiple platforms (security, networking, virtualization, Microsoft, etc...) who would consider this student an expert in whichever interface we are working in at that moment. It is the feeling of this student they see a professional who knows the ins and outs of whatever they are paying me for at that moment, the challenge however lies in the fact that this student is a technologist in the tail end of the 20th century and start of the 21st century. This is a time when technologies and standards are expanding at almost exponential rates. What this student feels is that it is most important to have foundation knowledge of whatever technology being interfaced with and understand not only the fundamentals but also the maximums and minimums. Understanding technologies is more than just the ability to set them up but the ability to support those same technologies when issues arise and stop an incident from becoming a problem. For IT people in the early half of the 21st century (and most professions) the learning process never stops.

It has been said that "a professional makes difficult things look easy." It is the opinion of this student that these technologies are finite systems created and certified by standard bodies (i.e.— IEEE). Maybe we make it look easy because we have mastery of this finite domain.

In conclusion this draft articulates the basis for an introduction to networking by describing the most basic LAN environment connecting to a WAN with special considerations for real time voice traffic and strong security posturing while highlighting best-business-practices in accord with industry standards and vendor requirements. The attached documentation illustrates the practical application and implementation components. This student thanks Strayer University for the opportunity to submit this experience portfolio.

References

Lammle, T. 2015. *CompTIA network+ study guide* (3rd ed.). Indianapolis, IN: John Wiley & Sons. Inc. (referenced the Table of Contents)

Supporting Documentation

Professional Documents

    Jonathan's Resume (written in 2014)

    Jonathan's Curriculum Vitae (*not exhaustive—written in 2008)

3 Letters of Verification

  Document Composition Examples

    MPLS Implementation Plan Overview

    VoIP H.323 Networking Integration Overview

    Disaster Recovery Implementation Overview

    Secure Network Proposal Example

Diagrams

    Global Secure LAN/WAN Diagram

    End-to-End QoS Diagram

INDEX

D

Data collection, 6–7, 91
Demonstrations, 92
Digital narrative, 91
Digital portfolios, 91
Documentation, 16–17
DSST, 93

E

Educational Testing Service (ETS), 1
English Composition, 36, 37
Ethics and personal integrity, 63
Experience, explicit knowledge with, 5
Experiential education, 52
Experiential learning, 5
    Kolb's model of, 5–8
    portfolio, 103
Explicit knowledge with experience, 5

F

Factual data collection, 11–12
Faculty and academic leadership, 54
Faculty assessors, payment of, 89. *See also*
    Assessors
Faculty-developed rubrics, 53–54
Faculty member, on portfolios and
    assessment, 58–59
Faculty subject matter experts, 4, 38
Feedback, 32, 38, 48
Fueling the Race to Postsecondary
    Success, xiii

G

GANTT Chart, 15, 19
Global Learning Qualifications Framework
    (GLQF), 92–93
Good assessor feedback, 48–49

H

Higher education, prior learning
    assessment for, 94

Host systems, 116
Human resource management
    course description, 77
    documentation, 83–85
    learning narratives, 77–82
    learning objectives, 77
    portfolio assessment, 101
    practices, 78
    rubric, 85

I

Innovation, 91
Integrity, 39
Internet-based distance learning, 104
Interpersonal processes, 62–63
Inter-rater reliability studies, 55
Introduction to Networking course
    background, 103–104
Introduction to Paralegal Studies
    assessment, 48
    assessor feedback, 48
    conclusion part, 44
    feedback on, 48
    introduction part
        background information, 39–40
        course presentation, 40
        statement of purpose and format, 41
        supporting documentation, 40, 45–47

K

Kolb's model of experiential learning, 5–8
    demonstrates, 26
    information gathering, 6–7
    learning objective, 6–8
    management in purchasing, 7–8

L

Leader attributes, 61–62
Leadership Theory and Practice II, Lead 310
    assessor feedback, 67
    conclusion, 64
    course description, 60–61
    documentation, 65–66

U

University of Maryland University College
  (UMUC), 94
UExcel, 93

V

Value engineering, 8, 14
Virtual Trunking Protocol, 110

W

Wireless access point (WAP), 111
Wireless network adapters, 111
Workshops for portfolios, 36

9 781524 913434